Modern Yacht Maintenance

Modern Yacht Maintenance

Loris Goring

DAVID McKAY COMPANY, INC.
New York

First American Edition, 1978

Library of Congress Catalog Card Number: 77-89156
ISBN 0-679-50829-5
Printed in Great Britain

Published in Great Britain by
Stanford Maritime Limited
12 Long Acre, London WC2E 9LP

To Cyril who introduced me to
fitting out in the Essex Marsh
in January snow and Don who
always insists on being master
anti-fouler in April
My thanks.

M.Y. 'Sea Hound of Dart'

Foreword and Acknowledgements

While writing this book I have kept firmly in my mind the average yachtsman owning a production motor or sail boat. This reader would, perhaps, be much like myself – able to admire the skills of the old-timer who poured boiling pitch into deck seams while his canvas sails boiled in a cauldron of preservative goo, but thankful for modern technology that has produced a good-looking, efficient boat with – dare I say it? – a minimum of maintenance involved. Perhaps the word 'minimum' might be questioned when the work programme I have outlined is checked over, but in my view, a great deal of unnecessary work can be avoided by sticking to a routine maintenance schedule. Neglect often means repairs using strong-arm tactics – and that really is work.

In the text, I have given weight to the care of things mechanical. Engines still tend to be neglected by both builders and owners, and since the engine installation is usually the most expensive single item apart from the hull, I feel this is justified.

I would like to acknowledge the help of all the companies whose products are mentioned in this book. Their technical information is invaluable and always freely available, not only to writers such as myself but to their customers. Nevertheless, the test of a product is in its use aboard a boat and I have no hesitation in recommending those mentioned, which I have used with pleasing results over a long period of time.

In particular I would like to thank Peter White of the Fredrick Mountford Corrosion Laboratory; Richard

Gatehouse for allowing me to publish his log calibration tables; Ratsey & Lapthorn for information about sails; A. C. Delco Europe, and indeed all those companies who have supplied the basis for some of the illustrations.

Loris J. W. Goring
Brixham, Devon.

List of Illustrations

Contents

Chapter 1
GENERAL PRINCIPLES OF YACHT MAINTENANCE

Although I might have been delighted if the publisher had asked me to write one of those 'Everything-you-want-to-know-about . . .' kind of books, such quantities of information would have produced a volume that would have immediately priced it beyond the reach of most yachtsmen. The whole point of this book is that it is for the boat owner who can't afford to be out sailing all summer, leaving maintenance jobs for someone else to do and footing the bill without a tremor.

Most of us have to struggle and save to buy a boat and struggle again to maintain it. Yet in a way this is part of the pleasure; it strengthens the pride of ownership. The battle against the ravages worn by sea, weather and time against the hull, engine, rigging and sails is a constant challenge. Satisfaction comes in the realisation that sound maintenance not only saves money – but a great deal of worry when at sea.

It's a sad fact, but some yachtsmen have to give up yachting simply because the family goes sour on the subject. Enthusiasm is not necessarily infectious. Graciously allowing one's wife to apply the anti-fouling and mop out the bilges, or confining her to the galley during prolonged cruising, can quench the spirit of the most loyal spouse. Equally, a small sea can look terrifying even from a moderately large boat. If something goes wrong on a difficult passage, this can be the last straw for an already unnerved family. It is so much better if boat-owning can be a real partnership for the family man, without all the unpleasant or dreary chores being confined to one section of the crew. And there will be a far greater sense of confidence if the boat is well-found and well-maintained, and the chances of a breakdown at sea kept to the very minimum. Remember, life can be lost through some little job being neglected or put off until later. Maybe 'later' will be too late.

You may be doubtful of your own ability to do all the maintenance jobs about a boat. Most of us, after all, have limitations. My own particular hate is plumbing. I know I only have to glance at a pipe compression joint that I have just tightened for it to start leaking. But I have learned to my cost that even experts make mistakes – that was when thirty-six out of forty joints newly connected by a professional sprayed water all over the galley. I would say that few maintenance jobs are beyond the dedicated amateur – but do think carefully before taking on a really big job such as rebuilding or re-engining.

Some yachtsmen enjoy working on a boat through a lifetime. They get their pleasure from using materials and tools, planning and preparing and altering – and not from actually getting afloat. Most of us like being on the water and our maintenance schedule is programmed solely to ensuring a sea-worthy craft on a limited budget.

It is important to realise that the maintenance of any yacht is directly proportional to the initial design and construction. A badly-designed engine installation will be murder to service. It will probably have grim access with no room to wield a spanner, causing the engineer to hang upside down from a floor beam in the best tradition of the orang-outang family. If the construction of interior parts of a yacht is of sub-standard materials, there will certainly be early maintenance problems which would have been non-existent if prime quality materials had been used in the first place. As yacht-building seems to be getting dominated by accountants rather than craftsmen, there can be a general lowering of standards which may save cash for the builder and initial buyer but be a false saving in the end for the owner who has to put things to rights. We all get mesmerised when we fall in love with the yacht of our dreams. Pity love is so often blind for we miss seeing the problems she is going to create for us if the love affair turns out to be prolonged. It really is disastrous when, after purchasing, our eyes are opened to a real bitch of a boat! Perhaps the services of a surveyor are worthwhile after all, but I have a sneaking feeling that because a glass reinforced plastic boat can't get rot, a goodly number of yachtsmen go to sea on something more closely resembling a white elephant than a boat. A real quality yacht, where the initial design is first-class and which uses first-class materials and fittings, will always be easier to maintain than one built on penny-pinching lines.

Whether you like maximising or minimising the time you spend maintaining your yacht, you must work out some kind of a maintenance schedule. There's no need to make yourself a nervous wreck looking for trouble every minute you are aboard, but there is much to be said for casting a beady eye over every part of the yacht whenever an opportunity occurs. If you have to go up the mast for some reason, you might just as well look at all the fittings, rigging and halyards while you are up there. Engine manufacturers usually ask the owner to check water levels in cooling systems and oil levels daily. I guess very few yachtsmen do this, but some very serious problems can be avoided if you detect the first signs of a failure before any real damage is done. Looking for spots of oil that should not be there may well save losing all the oil through a failing seal. A drop of water may give away a hose that has perished and might just jettison the engine's cooling water on the next outing.

Take the bother to use your eyes regularly and not just at fitting-out time. Your other senses should not be neglected either – they often are, because we seem to live in a world where only the visual is important; plastic foods insult our palate and nostrils, while noise pollution of one kind or another reduces our ability to detect small but significant noises. Use your sense of smell to detect inadequate ventilation, a leak of hot oil or the acrid one of melting PVC insulation on an electrical cable. Some skippers leave their ears on watch when they are themselves asleep. The smallest change in the noise of the wind in the sails and rigging has them out of their berth in a minute. The slightest change in the sound of mechanical noises has the same effect on me. Is the change in the sound the start of bearing failure, lack of lubrication, or is it something less significant? One thing is for certain; things that look as if they are wrong, smell wrong or sound wrong cannot and must not be dismissed.

In recent years, a start has been made by one or two yacht-builders to supply their customers with decent service and maintenance manuals. I think it is pretty disgraceful that for a product often costing tens of times that of a car we are not given a manual of similar quality to those supplied by car manufacturers. Even worse, the average yacht-builder loses all the leaflets supplied by the manufacturer of components built into the yacht, which often contain vital information. I write to manufacturers of every component I have aboard for replacement leaflets and keep them in a waterproof plastic case aboard. What a perfect world it would be for us if all technical leaflets were published in A4 or A5 sizes so we could pop them into a ring binder. This would at least overcome the excuse that small yacht production runs cannot justify the publication of a decent manual!

Chapter 2
CORROSION–ITS EFFECT ON MAINTENANCE

I make no apologies for putting this chapter early in the book. While you are reading these first sentences, about half a ton of ferrous metal has disappeared as rust in the United Kingdom. It is estimated that the bill in a single year in this country can be as much as £300 million. Part of that weight is from your own yacht and some of the cash comes from your pocket. If corrosion could be stopped, we should all be better off and yacht maintenance would be minimal, and for cosmetic reasons alone.

Metallurgy is a complex science, but it is important to understand the basic principles in the context of the marine environment and the effect on metals used in yacht construction, fittings and fastenings. We need to buy the right fittings, to have them correctly fitted and to know how to maintain them so that they do not fail. Failure, disappointment and perhaps injury are the rewards for the yachtsman who does not understand what he is buying. An unsuitable product or a good product used incorrectly can cause trouble. I would suggest that the classification societies have dubious ways of defining the metals used in yacht construction. They do not necessarily guarantee the service life stated, and since specific applications are not defined, this could lead to incorrect applications with unsatisfactory results. It is doubly important, therefore, that the yachtsman has a good understanding of the problem.

Put in its simplest terms, all the metal parts of a boat want to revert to the state they were in when they were first dug out of the ground. It is unfortunate that salt water is about the best environment to encourage the process. Boats on inland waterways will have less of a problem as fresh water is less corrosive than salt water.

The effect of sea-water is complicated because it contains many destructive elements. Metal salts, suspended solids and biological organisms each put weight behind the attack. They are further encouraged by dissolved and suspended gases present in the water. Oxygen, ammonia and hydrogen sulphide (the marina mud stench) all promote chemical activity which destroys metals. Chemical activity is itself related to temperature, so corrosion will be greater where water is at elevated temperatures. No need for you to go down to the Mediterranean – the local power station might be pumping out millions of gallons of water near your mooring. Even in a small tidal harbour it is not unusual to find sewer water elevating the temperature a degree or so compared to that outside its breakwater.

Above the waterline, metal fittings get well sprayed with salt water which dries and produces a nice concentrated sodium chloride (salt) solution when it gets a bit of dew on it. As if that were not bad enough, the materials from which yachts are built have a direct influence on the rate and type of corrosion. Thus, damp and saturated timber will act as an excellent conductor for electrical currents whether generated by electrolysis or from a stray current from a poor electrical installation. The electrical current will cause corrosive action that not only eats the fasteners away but can leave the timber in a soft, decaying condition.

One major problem with yachting today is that many of the gadgets the yachtsman is tempted to buy are not proper marine items. We are inundated with junk from the caravan and camping industry, bits and pieces left over from the car industry. While these products might be considered perfect for their original purpose, they are an extremely poor buy for the yachtsman. I am not saying that there are not first-class examples of products that have been competently 'marinised' for, heaven help us, where would we be without 'land' engines properly converted to marine engines? Here the manufacturers go to great lengths in their research to eliminate or at least minimise the effects of the environment on the performance of their engines. But beware of the numerous small items (with large price tags), which will soon corrode and fail in the marine environment. A protective plating such as cadmium which might be all right for an item used on your car will be eaten away in weeks when it is put on your yacht.

It is important that the yachtsman knows how to recognise corrosion in its various forms. The types of corrosion to look for are summarised below.

Bi-Metallic and Galvanic Corrosion

Sea-water, as we have said, is a strong electrolyte. That is, it serves as a path in the exchange of ions between two metals which then generate a potential between themselves. The potential difference between different metals when immersed in sea-water has been established as the Galvanic Series Table shown below. The current flows, resulting in the least noble metal (anode) being eaten away while the more noble (cathode) suffers little or no damage. We can now see how cathodic protection works. In many marine engines, there are small blocks of zinc, aluminium or magnesium which are purposely put there by the manufacturer to corrode away. Thus, the zinc block on the leg or propeller boss of the outboard will dissolve away in a season or less while the more noble aluminium casting is protected. Failure to renew cathodic protection blocks on underwater parts will lead to serious corrosion in castings, shafting, propellers, stern gear and skin fittings.

The Galvanic Series Table

Platinum, Gold
Titanium
Silver
Austenitic Stainless Steel (Passive)
Silver Solder
Monel
Cupro nickel

Bronzes, Copper
Brass
Tin
Lead
Austenitic Stainless Steel (Active)
Cast Iron
Steel
Aluminium
Cadmium
Zinc
Magnesium

Ideally, if we only used metals close to one another in the table we should have no serious problems, but cost, easy availability and sheer ignorance ensure that this basic rule is broken with inevitable results.

I should explain that stainless steel, which appears twice in the table, can be found in two conditions. Normally it protects itself from corrosive attack by a naturally generated oxidised surface. When in this condition it is said to be passive and more noble than the metals lower down the list. If for some reason this film is removed and is unable to replace itself, the stainless steel becomes active and will then be eaten away at frightening speed. It is nonsense to believe that stainless steel is the answer to every yacht design problem. Stainless steel becomes active when it is shielded from an oxygen supply as, for example, a screw embedded in wood, especially under water where chlorides in the sea-water penetrate the passive film. It is therefore recommended that stainless steel should never be used below the waterline.

The kind of place to look for shielding and crevice attack in stainless steels is where sea-water is readily available and oxygen is not. Look at stainless steel shafting where it runs through water seals on pumps. You will often find crevice attack where the seal bearing on the shaft has worn the oxidised surface to make it 'active' and the moisture running under the seal has started a vicious crevice attack which eats in a pitting way into the shaft and eventually makes it so rough that it chews up the rubber seal. Don't worry about the propeller shafting in this context because bearings are usually water-lubricated and receive a sufficient oxygen supply to renew film and remain passive.

Aluminium as a building, fabricating and casting material has a great deal to recommend it in the marine world. It is readily available in sheet, extrusions and casting billets, and designers find its high strength-to-weight ratio particularly attractive. Just think of the weight of an outboard if it was cast in iron rather than aluminium alloys! However, as it is so low in the Galvanic Series Table it demands special consideration. It is death to aluminium to have any copper alloys *near* it, never mind fastening it. Neither does it get on with steel. Every aspect of its use needs special consideration but when this is done, aluminium can provide a long-lasting material.

Anti-fouling systems must not contain copper salts and it is important that small areas of underwater aluminium which have their protective paint system abraded to expose the metal should be repainted at the earliest opportunity as a small anodic area will lead to serious corrosion. On the other hand, a large anode/small cathode situation is quite tolerable, so it is perfectly safe and advisable to use stainless steel fasteners to secure aluminium sheet in marine construction.

Since the corrosion so far discussed is an electro-chemical process, remember that the process will be accelerated at elevated temperatures and conversely will be slowed up at low temperatures. In a frozen canal a steel boat will not come to much harm, but in warm waters a much faster rate of corrosive decay will set in. As marine engines produce so much unwanted heat rather than energy delivered to the propeller, certain parts of them will be eaten away at an unhealthy rate - more about this later.

Stray Current Corrosion

The installation of yacht electrical systems is still, I am sorry to observe, of very low standard. Wiring is run in damp places, electrodes are left unsealed, switches placed in wet areas. It is, unfortunately, badly installed and badly maintained. One finds mixed earthing arrangements and even positive earthing being used, which should not be allowed on a boat. Even on a correctly negative earthed system there can be serious trouble.

One engine manufacturer changed the alternator isolating pad on his engines but it was not discovered until several propellers were eaten away beyond repair. The new material was allowing a stray current to surge down the propeller shafting, so making the propeller blades perfect sacrificial anodes! The answer is to keep the yacht's electrical system in tip-top order.

Stress Corrosion

This is not to be confused with the mechanical failure of a component after it has been eaten away by normal corrosive manifestation. It is a complex form of corrosion involving a combination of chemical attack, work hardening and heat transfer stresses which combine to make a normally ductile material behave in a brittle manner and fracture at much lower working stresses than would normally be expected. Usually, aluminium bronze, silicon bronze, carbon steel, stainless steel (18/8 and 18/10/3 types) and Monel 400 are not subject to stress corrosion in the yachting environment. We often find work hardening of copper piping in badly installed fuel systems which cause havoc when they fracture. Brass, when cold worked, will crack extensively and rapidly when exposed to, say, a small amount of ammonia in harbour water. I find it a source of worry that many yacht marinas are now tidal, having a sill that ensures a high concentration of yacht effluent in them for a period either side of low water. Such high concentration of pollutants is bound to have a deleterious effect on some yachts which are not properly protected against the ravages of sewage. Bronze propellers and skin fittings may be less affected but are not entirely immune.

Hot caustic alkali solutions will cause carbon steel to crack. I have seen it advised that heat exchangers should be cleaned with a caustic solution provided it is well washed out afterwards. The practice is not to be recommended.

Impingement Attack

Where water velocity washes corroded metal away as it impinges on it, the attack will be accelerated and can be a serious problem. To summarise, these are the steps that the yacht-builder and yachtsman can take to minimise the damage corrosion can do:

1. Try to use the more noble materials for construction and fastening and avoid mixing equal areas of metals which are well separated on the Galvanic Table.
2. You may use large anode/small cathode combinations (large sheet of aluminium fastened with stainless steel screws).
3. Dissimilar metals should always have isolating compounds and gaskets which will not allow the transfer of galvanic currents between them. Plastic films, silicon rubbers, hard rubber and plastic sleeves can all be used in specific applications and should be chosen for their durability and insulation factor when subject to the wetting they must inevitably undergo.
4. Check the electrical system and wiring as stray currents will cause corrosion havoc.
5. Be aware of situations which could enable stress corrosion to take place.
6. Cathodic protection is highly advisable, and if provided on parts of the boat's equipment must be maintained to a high standard at all times.

Performance of Materials & Fasteners

MATERIAL	TYPE	APPLICATION	SPECIAL REMARKS
Stainless Steel	18/8	Only for interior fittings or on fresh-water craft.	Never use below waterline – is subject to severe shielding attack (lack of oxygen). Fasteners used in dry interior situations give satisfactory results. Never use in damp – especially saline-damp – timber.
Stainless Steel	18/10/3 BS 316S16 Previously EN58J	Superior material for deck, mast, rigging and superstructure fitting. Electro-polishing gives superior but more costly high polish compared to machine polishing.	Molybdenum addition gives superior grade for casting and fasteners. Always to be preferred to 18/8. For long life, fitting the correct specification type is vital. Standard material for bolts.
Monel (Nickel-copper alloy)	Monel 400* *Trade name of Henry Wiggins & Co. Ltd.	Excellent resistance to sea-water. Most suitable and reliable for all fasteners in a vessel, even in contact with ferrous metals.	Most suitable for fixing components below the waterline into timber and GRP standard stock material for woodscrews and bolts. Good for keel bolts. Most expensive but should last a lifetime.
	Monel K 500	Same excellent corrosion resistance to 400 but much higher strength.	Stronger, harder and more wear-resistant for machine parts, especially shafting rigging and fasteners that are highly stressed.
Bronzes	Silicon Bronze (Copper-silicon alloy)	Good general purpose fastener material for boats. Fasteners suitable for use into timber immersed in sea-water.	Standard stock woodscrew and bolt material, very corrosion-resistant especially shielding attack. Not susceptible to dezincification (removal of zinc content by galvanic action within the fastener itself).
	Aluminium Bronze (Copper-aluminium alloy)	An alternative to silicon bronze. Used in Admiralty pump valves.	Marine fouling never occurs on copper alloys. Their corrosion rate is less than 0.001 in (0.025mm) per year.

...rior to the above two.

	Manganese bronze	Inferior castings which suffer severe attack in sea-water.	Misleadingly named. It is only a modified high strength brass with *poor* corrosion resistance in sea-water.
Brass	Ordinary	Widely used for woodscrews and bolts. Also referred to as 'yellow metal'. Acceptable for dry interior cabinet work. Appearance and corrosion resistance improved by nickel and chrome plating.	Severe dezincification takes place in damp timber and below waterline fastenings. Never use for submerged joints as woodscrews unless in dinghy which spends a lot of time out of water.
	Naval (60% copper, 39% zinc, 1% tin)	Used in some Admiralty equipment.	Tin increases resistance to dezincification but not recommended as failures can still arise. Proper bronzes are still to be recommended.
Aluminium alloys	Various. Usually unspecified	Deck and saloon fittings. Excellent grade for hull and superstructure available but *never use copper-rich anti-fouling paints* (severe galvanic attack).	Specifications from manufacturers lacking. Quality varies from excellent to disgusting. Never use copper alloys anywhere near aluminium. Never use copper bearing alloys (Duralumin H15) or free machining grades.
Gunmetal	Various	For casting fittings only. Not recommended for fasteners although sometimes found in this application.	Castings have good resistance to corrosion in sea-water.
Carbon Steel		Working vessels, larger yachts, inland waterways craft. Fittings and fabrications often zinc or cadmium plated.	Anodic coatings – zinc and cadmium have limited wear before corrosion takes place in sea-water. Cathodic coatings create rusting in baser steel. Never use steel screws in holes previously occupied by copper ones. Steel can be well protected from corrosion by use of high performance paint systems.
	PTFE coated } Epoxy sprayed }	Lower cost than equivalent S/S fasteners.	New development from oil rig industry. Proving very successful in extreme environments.

Chapter 3
PAINTING AND VARNISHING

Paint and varnish have two functions: to protect and to beautify. Cosmetics are important for they create an attractive and protective surface. On the other hand, they can cover a multitude of sins! With an eye to minimising corrosion, it is vital to select the correct materials and then protect them with a coating which acts as a barrier to the elements set on destruction.

The first question the boat owner asks is 'Which is the best make of paint?' The glib answer is 'A marine one'. You see, paints are formulated to protect against specific environments. It stands to reason that, like everything else used on a boat, the paint will have to be pretty good to stand up to salt, sun, ultra-violet light, abrasion and fuel oils to name but a few! To save a few pence, some yachtsmen think that the odd bits of paint left over from household use will do, as these paints are cheaper than proper marine ones. At best, this paint will give a second rate performance and at worst will cause you to do a lot more painting work for a dangerously low rate of protection.

Two international companies whose marine paints I have no hesitation in recommending are 'International Yacht Paints', and 'Little Ship Paints'. Both companies have a very complete range of marine paints which have been produced to meet exacting standards and both produce excellent guides for either amateur or professional yacht painters. I believe it is most important for the owner to have at his fingertips the most comprehensive information available, as yacht-painting has become an art based on most exacting technology.

There is such a wide choice of materials available that if we simply wander along to the chandlers with a vague request for a tin of paint for fitting-out, we are likely to get a long sales talk and quite possibly the wrong paint. The fact is, each can of paint is tailor-made for a specific application. The paint technologist is working in an industry where he is almost daily inundated with new or superior ultra-violet stable pigments, more durable resins and better paint additives which are going to make for a better coating wherever it is applied. Don't let this technology frighten you, because the literature and the labelling on the cans tells you precisely how, when and where to apply the coatings, the right order and gives correct drying times between. Even cleaning the brush is more scientific these days, as different paints have different solvents. Disobeying the specific rules of painting with modern materials could land you in some real trouble. Take for example the yachtsman painting with the help of his dolly-bird. She was painting the topsides with a two-can polyurethane paint system - but she forgot to stir in the second can which hardens the paint. That yachtsman forgot his manners when the topsides just became a treacly mass which refused to dry.

Types of Coating

Basically, two types are available. The first, referred to as 'conventional' types - with which we are familiar for general use - are paints and varnishes which dry in contact with air which oxidises them and evaporates their solvents. These paints used to be made of natural oils and resins, but today they are a complex mixture of natural and synthetic resins and oils and are therefore generally referred to as 'synthetics'. Their beauty is in their simplicity. They are easier to apply, less demanding in mixing preparation and although extremes of weather, especially temperature, are still to be avoided, they put up with more fickle fitting-out weather than the high-performance system.

Some confusion has been caused in yachtsmen's minds with the introduction of 'one-can polyurethanes': these are not high-performance paints and varnishes, as their chemical reaction is allied to that of conventional paints rather than proper 'two-can' polyurethanes, where chemical reaction between the hardener and the base takes place. This, the second type of painting system, is the 'high performance' one as the chemical reaction is really one of 'cure', the final coating being far superior in strength, abrasion resistance and long-term weathering performance. This superior performance has to be paid for in that the surfaces require much more careful preparation, the mixing and overcoating are critical and you need good weather when the cure time is directly linked to the ambient air temperature. The evaporation of the solvents is comparatively speedy and the touch-dry stage not so far behind. However, the chemical reaction, though initially quick, may take as long as seven days to reach full cure and maximum hardness.

The high-performance paints are in two types – the polyurethane and the epoxy systems. Like the polyurethanes, the epoxy systems are two-pot but they are very limited in colour range – white, light blue and 'tar' black – but they do offer outstanding performance in water, abrasion and chemical resistance, and can be used as a base for sheathing the bottoms of wooden craft to provide an impenetrable barrier against marine borers. I believe the two-can epoxy system will have much to offer the yachtsman whose glass reinforced plastic boat has become subject to 'boat pox', of which more anon.

Compatibility

The four basic paint systems, conventional synthetics, one-can polyurethanes, two-can high performance polyurethanes and two-can epoxy coatings, have different types of solvent and thinners. A major problem is one of compatibility. It's a terrifying thought to imagine the new coat of paint suddenly beginning to lift and blister over a large area before the stuff is dry. But there is no real need to worry for each paint firm advises specifically on the compatibility of its products and when it fails to mention a rival's product, or you have no idea what is already on the part of the yacht you wish to paint, you have to resort to a little testing. Try the thinners of the new paint system you wish to use on the old paint substrata. If there is a reaction, two possible courses are open to overcome it. One can either remove the substratum completely or seal it off. Removing it can be by means of a chemical paint stripper, blow-lamp or mechanical abrasion. There are now chemical paint strippers formulated for use on GRP yachts, but be absolutely certain that they are compatible or the normal paint strippers available will seriously damage a GRP surface. Blow-lamps must only be used for stripping a surface on wood which is to be painted and should not be used on wood that is to be varnished as scorch marks will show. (*NEVER* use a blow-lamp on GRP!) Over a long period of time, with craft built of various materials, I have my own preferences for types of coatings; they have no scientific basis but are just from my own observation and perhaps prejudice.

Preference in Paint Systems

For wooden yachts I prefer conventional paint systems and, where appropriate, ordinary varnish. I believe wood breathes and certainly its moisture content varies enormously through the season and from one plank to the next. The deck may be roasting in the sun while the topsides are splashed cool and the bottom is well saturated below the waterline. There is, therefore, always a deal of movement in wood as the moisture content varies. This moisture needs to escape or it builds up a vapour pressure under a paint film and blisters are the result, with eventual paint failure. Two-can polyurethanes are much more (but not perfectly) waterproof and thus there is a greater chance of vapour lift if the moisture does manage to get into the timber, perhaps through mechanical damage to the paint surface.

On more stable surfaces such as steel, aluminium or GRP, I would certainly go for high-performance paint systems every time, as here the more waterproof the coating can be made the better. With metal hulls we are not going to have any vapour content to worry about.

Contrary to popular opinion, glass reinforced plastics are not 'waterproof' but slowly absorb a small amount of water when they are immersed. It is difficult to know why the misunderstanding first arose that resins were impermeable but let us kill that one stone dead. The great shame is that we have known for many years that permeability in GRP can be reduced below the waterline by using an unfilled, non-coloured - i.e. clear - resin for the gel coat. Quality moulders and those complying with Lloyds rules do this, but how often do we find all the boats at a boat show with coloured resin bottoms or more usually anti-fouled so that we cannot see what has gone on underneath at all?

I believe the answer to water absorption is a first-class two-can epoxy system applied when the craft is new, as it is the most waterproof of all the systems. This is certainly needed on old GRP craft but application should only be undertaken when the hull has been ashore some time so that it has rid itself of at least a high proportion of the water it has absorbed. One winter under-cover and an epoxy system applied on a hot, late spring day might save a deal of GRP trouble for older yachts.

The two-can polyurethanes are certainly my favourite for stable topsides and superstructures. On GRP the polyurethane is really related chemically to the gel coat; what better, then, to renew the gel coat when it is getting jaded?

Now, armed with the paint manufacturer's guide, we can choose the paint systems we prefer - either conventional or high-performance - test for compatibility and take any action necessary before we really get down to producing that desirable super finish.

Safety with Paints

There can be two hazards with paints - fire and health. Paints contain organic solvents which will easily catch fire when exposed to naked flames, sparks or even by spontaneous ignition when left lying around. These risks should be guarded against and if fire should occur it must only be fought with a fire blanket, carbon dioxide powder or BCF extinguishers - NEVER WATER. It is always advisable to protect eyes, hands, face and any exposed skin areas from paint. It is most sensible to protect them from high-performance systems and anti-foulings as these contain either potential skin irritants or poisons. The following will help avoid any problems for your health.

1. Always read the label on the paint can: it will advise fully if there are fire or health risks.
2. Paint in properly ventilated spaces so that breathing of solvent vapours is minimised. Wear a cartridge type respirator when abrading old anti-fouling. All anti-foulings contain poison.
3. Wear barrier cream or disposable polythene gloves on hands.
4. Always clean up yourself and your boat before eating or smoking.
5. Protect your head and hair from overhead painting splashes.

Tools for Painting

1. Abrasive papers. Dry glasspaper or garnet paper for varnish surfaces and final cutting back. 'Wet and dry' papers used wet for heavy cutting back. Electric sanders must use only dry papers or you will be electrocuted. 'Wet and dry' 120 grade is coarse, 240 grade medium and 400 fine. I find these three are all that are wanted, although a really fine burnish may require a 600 paper followed by a burnishing compound.
2. An electric sander for wood is highly recommended, but it will not get into small corners. A cork rubbing block to wrap the paper around will. Cut papers to size – don't tear them.
3. Plenty of clean rags. One should always be to hand for mopping up the odd splash and another as a 'tack rag'. The tack rag is made slightly sticky with a minute amount of thinner and paint or varnish from the system you are using so that bits on the surface are lifted off to obtain a perfect finish. Never paint immediately after sanding or after using a tack rag, as the surface will be attacked and checking (crocodile skin) may occur. A couple of hours will allow the surface to settle down and all solvent to evaporate.
4. A selection of brushes ½in to 4in (1.3 cm to 10cm). Buy the best you can afford as they will last a long time if properly cared for and will always give a superior finish to your work. Large areas need a large brush.

5. Brush cleaners. Each painting system will recommend the correct type. Cleaners are not necessarily 'thinners': read the paint manufacturer's instruction on this point. After cleaning brushes in the correct solvent, either suspend them in a jar of the same material if they are to be used again, or wash them out thoroughly with detergent and water. Rinse thoroughly and hang up to dry. 'Thinners' are seldom needed for use when brush painting, but may be necessary for sprayed applications: manufacturers formulate paint of the correct consistency for brushing, but spraying may require a thinner mix.
6. Blow-lamps or torches. For small areas of wood (NEVER GRP!) a paraffin blow-lamp is not tiresome, but where large areas are to be stripped it is heavy on the wrist. The small portable gas torch is light and effective. For really large areas, the large cylinder of gas attached by flexible gas pipes to a lightweight torch is ideal. Always have a fire extinguisher immediately to hand when using blow-lamps.
7. Water, degreasing solvent and detergents. Surfaces to be painted must be as near perfectly clean as possible. Salt and grease will ruin the chances of a good painting job. When water is used, allow plenty of time for the surface to dry off thoroughly.
8. Selection of scrapers and sharpening file, trowelling and filling knives.

Most marine paints are formulated so that they can, if thinned, be sprayed. Undoubtedly, as yachtsmen demand a finish on their yachts akin to that on their new cars, we will see more and more air and airless spraying taking place. Its inclusion here is perhaps premature, as often boats are laid up so close to one another that there could be complaints from the owners of surrounding boats. If you have no such problems, I would recommend you to find out more about airless spraying units which are driven by electricity. These are comparatively inexpensive, being a self-contained unit and not requiring a separate compressor.

How Much Paint?

Your paint manufacturer will give data on the covering rate

for each specific paint he makes. Use the following formulae:

Area of Topsides	= (Overall length + Beam) × 2 for average freeboard.
Area of Decks	= (O.A. Length × Beam × 0.75) - area taken up by coachroof, hatches and cockpit.
Area for Bottoms	= L.W.L. × (Beam + Draft).*
Area of Spars	= 7.14 × diameter × height.

* For full-bodied craft such as motor cruisers and sailboats with straight keels and straight stems. Reduce by 25 per cent for sailboats with overhangs fore and aft and by 50 per cent for slim racing craft with fin keels.

Note quantities of paint used in log book so that the correct quantities may be ordered the next season.

Hints are given on painting in later chapters, but before this, a word about basic procedures and what they will achieve.

Preparation

The finished work will only be as good as the preparation of the surfaces to be painted. After laying up a boat, there will be dirt streaks down the topsides, blown debris and dust on the decks, so the first job is to remove the winter covers and give a thorough wash down with fresh clean water with a little detergent added. Dry glass-papering surfaces not only evens them up but will help the new coats of paint to adhere to wood and metal. Plastic boats of any kind (GRP and expanded polystyrene) should never receive mechanical abrasion to their surfaces unless they are to have paint coats applied, and then only with care so that the gel coat substrata is not cut into. Rubbing down is a long, hard process and it seems so negative making the boat look worse and covered in paint dust again, but at least when it is done you are well on the way to making the yacht pristine, so cheer up.

Priming

These are the very first coatings put onto previously unpainted surfaces. Their function is to give a first-class adhesion between the surface and the undercoat. Each substrata must have its own special undercoat and often more than one coat is recommended. They are often thinned down for the first coat where the substrata will allow them to penetrate to a greater depth. Epoxy primers may be regarded as multi-purpose, as they are happy on all substrata except where a copper-based wood preservative can interfere with this family of coatings. Metals need etching primers where an acid is often employed to eat minute pits into the surface, so giving the next coat of paint a greater degree of adhesion. Underwater priming not only has to provide the adhesion for following coats, but also acts as the real moisture barrier to seal the surface.

Stopping and Fillers

Their job is to even up the surfaces. Like the paint systems, they may be based on conventional materials or from the epoxy high-performance materials.

The epoxy fillers are highly regarded as they are solvent-free and therefore do not shrink. Being a two-pack product, they must be mixed accurately and will have a defined 'pot life' which means they will, after a stated time, be useless for further working. They can be used on bare substrata previous to priming because of their high adhesive factor, but they must be put onto a compatible primed surface.

Conventional fillers may be waterproof or not. They are designed to be used only in relatively thin layers and primed as they are built up. Building up and rubbing down can be a long, tedious business, but thicker films may crack and cause later blistering when the oils they contain do not oxidise properly or solvent becomes trapped.

Stopping is filler that is rather thicker for filling major defects. A demand for quantities of stopper usually denotes a poor construction.

Always finish off over the top of filled or stopped areas with another coat of primer.

Brush fillers contain sufficient solvent to allow them to be brushed into small surface imperfections.

Undercoating

Undercoats are now only associated with conventional paint systems, and when the correct priming has been used they are optional. However, they are useful for obliterating colours when a change is desired, and I always feel they give a greater depth of colour or a more lustrous white when they are used.

Finishing Coats

For perfection, we can do no better than imitate the work of the coach painter. A deep rich gloss can only be achieved by the meticulous application of four or five coats and 'denibbing' between all except the final coat. (Denibbing is the light rubbing down with a fine abrasive, used either wet or dry, to remove bits of blown grit and dust on the surface and provide the fine key for the next coat. Papers of 320 or 400 grit are ideal for this job.) This is a council of perfection and the majority of owners will be hard put to go as far as two finishing coats. Two coats will be quite enough if you want to prevent too much paint build-up and the job is done each year. For yachts where paint and varnish has to last, five coats have been known to last five years without failure.

Fire Retardent Paint Systems

These are generally based on conventional paint systems and can be decorative or not according to the product chosen. Usually the paint contains antimony oxide or other antimony compounds with strong fire retarding properties. I have found that the weathering of antimony-filled paints is not as good as normal undercoat/gloss systems, but nevertheless I would have no hesitation in recommending them for interior painting of yachts. At the time of writing, there are no fire retardent varnishes that I can recommend, as those available do not stand up to the marine environment.

Varnishing

No finish on a boat can be, in my opinion, more beautiful than perfectly varnished natural timber. Well done, it is the acme of the painter's art; badly done and neglected it makes any boat a sorry sight. Four types of material are available and sold as yacht varnishes.

1. Phenolic resin-based varnishes give a really rich, lustrous finish to brightwork. This is a conventional finish which will darken with age and may incorporate a UV filtering agent which stops the wood from bleaching.

2. Alkyd resin varnish does not stain or darken but is very pale. It is more water permeable than the phenolic, and I would recommend its use only where the owner wanted to keep the natural colour of the timber in the boat's interior cabin spaces.

3. One-can polyurethane varnishes do not discolour but allow some bleaching of the timber. They lack the lustre of the first type and have, I believe, little to recommend them.

4. Two-can polyurethanes are extremely waterproof and much harder than any other varnishes. They are clear and do allow a little bleaching of the substrata. They offer a first-class protection for really stable wood surfaces such as plywood, cold-moulded and hot-moulded hulls but should not be used where there is likely to be movement. If moisture, which has perhaps entered through a damaged area, gets under the varnish, vapour pressure on a hot day will lift the tough film off the substrata. Being two-can, it is more irksome to touch up scratches. Do not try to apply them on top of conventional varnishes.

Varnishing hints

The first coat onto bare wood is always well thinned with 25 per cent thinner added so that it soaks into the timber. Stir two-can varnish and allow to stand as air bubbles are a curse. For this reason don't stir conventional varnish, don't overbrush and don't scrape the bubbles off the brush onto the side of the can. At least five or six coats should be given to new wood and a minimum of two coats when re-varnishing. Teak is oily and should have a strong solvent (such as two-can thinners) applied to rid it of some of the suıface oil before coating.

Dust and debris from your woolly hat and jumper will ruin the finish. So will a neighbouring yachtsman sanding down or other air-borne dust. Scatter water widely over the surrounding ground to keep dust down. Choose a windless day with quick drying conditions. Take small cabin and cockpit items home and varnish in, ideally, covered accommodation.

Varnish is thinner than paint coat for coat when it is dry, so if you are going to burnish a two-can varnish give it a couple of extra coats to those I recommend. Always touch up mechanically damaged areas immediately - this will save blackening of the timber. Blackened timber can be restored by painting a warm solution of oxalic acid onto the wood. After bleaching, wash off with clean fresh water and allow to dry before priming. Oxalic acid is poisonous so take care.

Varnish for decks can be made non-slip by sprinkling the penultimate coat with silver sand while it is still tacky. Then after drying and removal of the excess sand, give a final coat of varnish.

Cabinet Finishes

Fine interior cabinet work can have a melamine finish as used by the furniture industry. These finishes are easy to apply, showing no brush marks, dry in 15 minutes or so and can be buffed down with steel wool to give a matt finish. They do give off highly unpleasant vapours, so really first-class ventilation is vital when they are being used. They are clear, do not darken with age and look extremely pleasant. A light rubbing down and re-coat is all that is necessary to restore them.

Anti-fouling

This is usually a hoary old chestnut for the yachting writer, but the simple truth is that their aim is to stop small sea creatures eating into wooden boats and to keep all sorts of sea plants and creatures from sitting on the under-water surfaces where they increase in size and slow the boat down. Like so many things on a boat, the amount of money you pay is normally proportional to the protection given or the quality of the product. It is therefore a waste of money to put an expensive anti-fouling on a boat that is to be used where fouling is light and conversely, it will be very expensive to put a light duty anti-fouling on a boat that is going into tropical waters or for a round the world voyage. The paint manufacturers offer excellent advice on their ranges of anti-foulings, but do make sure you enquire what paint substrata they recommend their anti-fouling to go on. To kill off the animals and plants, the anti-foulings contain a multitude of first class poisons, some based on arsenical and mercury compounds. Do read the application instructions from the manufacturer if you don't want to poison your best friend who is slapping the stuff on under the boat!

Just like a garden, the sea garden the underside of a boat provides will vary its growth rate from season to season. Have a good look at what other yachtsmen are using in the area you moor your boat and see what kind of fouling they are getting. If your boats sits for long periods on its mooring or you like a really long season well into the autumn, get a top quality anti-fouling. Like witch doctors' potions, paint manufacturers provide endless fun for experimentation when they almost annually produce a new brew that is the answer to the yachtsman's prayer – the damnation of weeds and animals that like boats. The really amazing thing is, the weeds and animals continue to flourish.

Sea creatures that eat wood are:

Ship-worm of many types but best known one is the Teredo. Enters timber below the waterline making small hole. It then turns and bores along the grain of the timber.

Martesia is a torpedo shaped mollusc that has a devastating effect. It excavates a burrow in timber and as it enjoys the company of Teredo the friendship can be catastrophic.

Gribble may be likened to a small maritime wood-louse which enjoys pulping unprotected underwater wood surfaces.

Chapter 4
HULL MAINTENANCE

There is, unfortunately, no material used in yacht construction that does not require maintenance. It is a great pity that when glass reinforced plastic was first introduced a great deal of misleading publicity claimed that it 'only needed washing down and never needed painting'. The hard fact is that, over a period of time, every single item on a yacht - including the hull - will need maintenance to repair damage caused by general use and the ravages of weather.

A designer has to recognise the qualities of the materials to be used in his designs, to ensure that their strengths and weaknesses are catered for. Equally, the boat owner must know something of these so that, before buying a boat, he can see that the design utilises the best features of the materials and minimises its limitations. A well-designed, well-built yacht will last a long time and be relatively easy to maintain compared to one of inferior design and construction.

Another major misconception is that with modern materials and boat production techniques, any unskilled slipshod labourer working in poor conditions can throw a boat together. I shall come back to this point when discussing GRP hulls, but be warned: a poorly built boat will have to be paid for later by the unfortunate owner. Bad practices may save a few pence for the builder, but may cost the owner pounds later on.

Wood construction

This splendid traditional material seemed in danger of being overshadowed when GRP 'en masse' was introduced in the 1960s. However, wood has staged something of a comeback

ROTS AND THEIR RECOGNITION

Name	*Appearance*
Dry Rot Merulius Lacrymans	1 Fluffy white masses often with yellow patches 2 Matted grey skin tinged yellow or lilac 3 Thin branching grey strands Fruit body like flat pancakes with white edges, brick red centre found when outbreak is extensive. *Wood* dry and brittle, generally light brown with deep cracks across the grain into brick-shaped pieces. Although initial development of this fungus needs temperate damp conditions, it will spread to dry sound timber quickly.
Wet Rots	
Poria Xantha most common but there are several other types of wet rot that can occur on wooden craft	Usually fine strand-like mycelium yellow or whitish in colour but not always present. Generally, woods become darker and main cracking occurs with the grain.

General Recognition Signs

1. Nasty musty smell when yacht is opened up.
2. Timbers and panelling curving outwards as they warp.
3. Any cracking, especially across the grain.
4. Any form of growth on wood or nearby surfaces.
5. Any softening of timber with easy penetration of a blunted point.
6. Timber that sounds 'dull' when struck.
7. Lifting paint and discolouration under varnish.
8. Structural failure of any wood.
9. Fasteners, deck fitting, keel bolt loosening unduly.
10. Red dust, nodular outgrowths, which become hard and chalky.

recently. Many of the traditional builders are doing well and, indeed, the ownership of a wooden yacht has in some parts of the world become a status symbol.

Wood is a wonderful material to work with. It has a high strength-to-weight ratio, is readily available practically anywhere in the world and is still better understood by the average man than any of the modern materials. Its limitations are that it will absorb water, is attacked by land and sea creatures, and it rots. Good maintenance can keep all these at bay so that the boat lasts for many years.

The sea-creatures that eat wood are dealt with in the section on anti-fouling (page 26).

Timber used in modern yacht construction is kiln dried to a precise moisture content. It is delivered to the builders from sawmills, but may be left lying around and so absorb water from the air. This hygroscopic action may affect the quality of glue lines, the absorption of timber preservatives and the endurance quality of the varnishing and painting. Once afloat, a boat will be pretty damp below the waterline from sea-water and above from spray and rain. Wood should have a low moisture content to keep it free from cracking, twisting and warping. Too much water of the wrong kind will destroy it. The table opposite lists the types of rot and their recognition.

Where to look for rots

A yacht that is really well sea-water-soaked with great use would probably never experience rot, for salt water is itself a rot inhibitor. The trouble comes from rainwater seeping into the wrong places, condensation and a lack of proper ventilation. Only a regular inspection of each part of the yacht as shown in Fig. 1 will ensure that rots have not got a stranglehold. For goodness sake, if you do go digging around your hull with a sharp point to test for softness, repair the damage with a spot of paint or that hole could be the seed bed for a galloping fungus!

What to do about rots if you find them

Dry rot spells death to a boat unless it is minutely rooted out and every surface sterilised. It often means a virtual rebuild, entailing the removal of all panelling and every single normally inaccessible place. Try to skip one area and a hiding fungus will set up a repeated attack which will undo all your

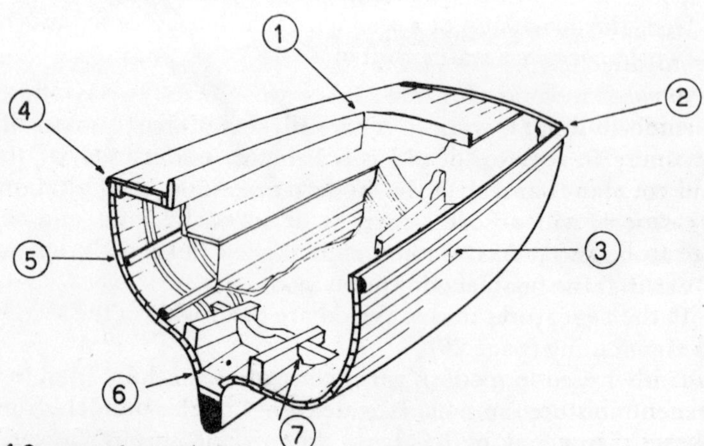

1. Corners of coamings.
2. Quarter knees.
3. Any scarph or butt joint.
4. Rubbing strake.
5. Stringers if lodging water.
6. Land of garboard strake.
7. Limber holes.
8. Under any deck fitting.
9. Stem and planking lands.
10. Corners of coachroof.
11. Around window and ports.
12. Under quadrant strips
13. Corners of hatches.
14. Behind fixed panelling.
15. Unventilated locker spaces.
16. Bottom of chain locker.
17. Around keel bolts.

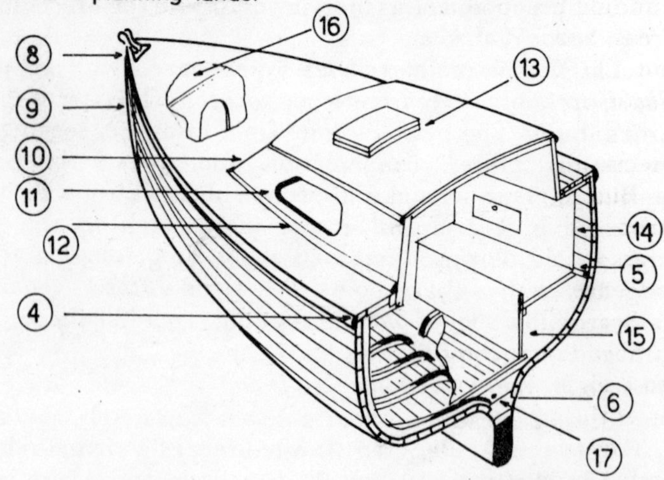

Fig.1. Where to look for wood rot.

work within months. You must be ruthless! Centres of attack must have all wood cut completely away at least 18in (46cm) from any centre. Wood that is still sound must have paint removed and be impregnated with a dry rot inhibiting chemical. On wood that is not to be revarnished I would recommend removal of paint with a blow-lamp. This will also kill rot spores and dry out the timber so that later chemical treatment can soak well into the wood. Where marine glues are to be used, do the wood repair involving the gluing first and then treat with chemicals which might otherwise interfere with the quality of the glue-line.

Wet rots

No, it's no good filling them with putty, plastic padding or cement and hoping they go away! You must accept that rot is always discovered at the last and worst moment, just as you investigate why the last perfect gloss coat of spring seems to be lifting off in that inviting sunshine. Again, cutting back to sound timber is needed, but since this rot does not spread over and into sound timber in the manner of dry rot, you will be relieved to know that the boat has no need to be torn apart and blasted with flame. Once the rotted sections of timber have been removed it is a case of following the normal boat-building practices and setting in new timber to the damaged areas. Space does not permit me to go into construction detail but Lloyds *Rules and Regulations for the Construction and Classification of Wood and Composite Yachts* and K. H. C. Jurd's *Yacht Construction* published by Adlard Coles offer precise advice. My own guidelines are as follows.

1. Butt joints on lengths of timber should have sturdy backing straps which are short of adjoining frames and have bevelled edges so that all-round drainage is provided and no water can lodge between strap and frame.
2. Scarph joints should be arranged to come in way of frames or have extra straps backing them. Scarph joints should be at least eight times the hull thickness and backing straps ten times the hull thickness.
3. Any timber inserted must not be such a tight fit that it puts undue pressure on surrounding timber or leaves insufficient space for a proper glue-line.
4. Only marine timber glues should be used for any repair.

5. Don't be afraid to call in the professional to do really difficult tasks such as replacing a garboard strake or inserting a new long plank in a clinker construction.
6. All completed repairs should be treated with a chemical wood preservative based on BS3452 or BS3453, the former being waterborne fixed salt type based on copper-chrome or copper-chrome-arsenic types, and the latter on organic solvent types such as naphthenates of zinc and copper and pentachlorophenol. The copper-based products tend to be green but can be painted over provided they are sealed off with a proper undercoat, whilst the pentachlorophenol-based ones are clear and thus ideal where they are to show through varnish.
7. Use the same type of fastener material for the repair that is already being used in the construction. (See Chapter 2 and note that steel screws put into holes previously occupied by copper ones will result in instant corrosion!)
8. If you are going to use plywood, make certain it is a correct marine grade and in the UK up to BS1088. Plenty of 'rubbish' plywoods are around these days and I have even found BS1088 stamped on foreign boards which could not possibly have conformed to the British Standard. The Trade Descriptions Act gives protection to the consumer in the UK, but compensation may not seem so good if the inferior wood calls for drastic renewals and repairs because it has failed after a short life. The problem with marine plywoods is that inferior boards have poor quality core material which is guaranteed to rot after a short life, and the core has 'gaps' which allow penetrating water to spread right across the core to start rot over large areas. Edges of plywood are most vulnerable to weather penetration and must always be protected.

Marine adhesives

A specialised subject and a highly technical one, but the manufacturers of marine adhesives are to be congratulated on the wide range of products that are now available to the amateur, and the technical literature which allows them to be used correctly. Two firms in the UK that will furnish fuller technical information on their products are: Borden Chemical Company (UK) Ltd., and C.I.B.A. (ARL) Ltd.

Resorcinol resin glues have outstanding durability in marine conditions (BS1204 weather and boil proof) and are ideal for multi-skin construction, laminating frames, knees, masts, etc. They will bond laminated plastics to wood far better than contact adhesives since the latter are not durable in marine use; teak can be bonded easily without the usual problems caused by the oil in the wood. They are two-part products consisting of a red liquid base and a powder hardener. The mixed adhesive will therefore stain fine cabinet work and is not to be recommended for that application. The Borden product under their 'Cascophen Resorcinol Glue' label is also used for their special yacht sheathing process 'Cascover' - nylon sheathing which gives wonderful protection below the waterline on wooden craft. For any shipwrighting job in wood which is later to be painted over, these glues are highly recommended. If you are careful to clean off the glue-line immediately with a wet cloth, you can prevent serious staining so that varnishing is possible. Aerodux is the C.I.B.A. equivalent.

Urea-Formaldehyde glues are only moisture-resistant but are still good for dinghy construction, where the boat is kept out of water for most of its days, and for fine interior cabinet work where staining is unacceptable. C.I.B.A. 'Aerolite 300' is a formulation using a liquid base spread on one surface to be jointed and a liquid hardener on the other. On bringing the two into contact, the necessary chemical reaction is set off and the glue hardens and sets. Borden 'Cascamite' is a 'one shot' powder product which is simply mixed with water. Glue-lines are easily cleaned up using a cloth and water, as are all brushes used, for all the glues mentioned so far are easily cleaned if they are washed out thoroughly in cold water immediately after use.

Melamine/Urea Formaldehyde glues are a modification of the former type and have better endurance, passing the BS1204 boil test. Timber preservative can affect all glues, so treatment is most safely done after the glue has had time to dry.

Epoxy resins - a superlative family of adhesives now formulated for just about every marine application you can think of. They will literally glue anything to anything else, giving immensely strong, weather-proof joints. They have but one snag – they are expensive. Both companies mentioned have a very extensive range of epoxy adhesives ranging from thin laminating resins to heavy putties which set like iron. They are two-pot systems consisting of base and hardener. Borden have a range which includes

a. Shaping and fairing in wood, metal and GRP for coachroofs, decks and hulls.

b. Bonding timber to GRP surfaces.

c. Bonding GRP decks and superstructures to GRP hulls.

d. General purpose bonding and repairs to wood and GRP, bulkheads, fitted furniture and cabinet work (non-staining).

e. Gap and hole filling and fairing-in metal keels, repairs to leaking pipes in emergency situations.

f. Anti-skid surfacing on GRP, timber and steel decks.

Safety with synthetic resins and epoxy adhesives is a simple matter of following the makers' directions. These products can, if used carelessly, give rise to skin complaints, but as the resins are easily washed off and barrier creams are available to give protection against the epoxys, it boils down to sensible hygiene being practised.

Sealants are part of the weaponry the yachtsman needs to understand in his boat preservation battle. They are used for a variety of applications including bedding skin fittings and valves, gap-sealing rubber fendering, bedding for deck fittings, caulking for plank-laid decks and general sealants for edges of joints on a variety of materials. They will be used on aluminium and steel hulls as isolating compounds between fittings of different metals and a seal for making watertight joints in plating, fittings and structures bolted onto the hull. Adshead Ratcliffe & Co Ltd specialise in a full range of modern sealants, and the Dow Corning Corporation in the USA provides a similar service there.

Polysulphide (two component) A.R. 'Arbokol 2175' is specially formulated to be used as a deck caulking sealant. Planking gaps must be thoroughly cleaned and perfectly dry before priming with Arbo Primer 327. Oakum or cotton caulking may be left in place so long as there is a 6–10mm seam depth. New caulking must be done in cotton as it has no tar content like oakum. The two parts of sealant are mixed and used immediately, poured into the seams or injected using a caulking gun. Joints should be slightly overfilled and when the cure is complete (in about twenty-four hours) cut off the excess with a sharp chisel flush with the deck. The 2150 grade is thicker and cannot be poured and is ideal for deck and skin fittings. These sealants have wonderful weathering properties and are quite immune from contamination to be found on boats.

Polysulphide (single component) A.R. 'Arbokol 1000', supplied in a ready-to-use cartridge, is suitable for sealing deck and skin fittings and bedding and bonding all types of deck fittings where a fast cure is not wanted. They accommodate movement and have good resistance to water, fuels and oils.

Silicone rubber sealant (one component) A.R. 'Arbosil 1081' has excellent adhesion properties on GRP, wood and aluminium. Good for hull and deck joints in bolted GRP assembly, sealing aluminium ports into GRP and aluminium, and general sealing of joints that are exposed and not to be painted.

Butyl (one component) 'Arbomast G.P.' is an oil-based sealing compound for general purpose caulking applications above the waterline where joints are to be painted. Particularly applicable to wooden structures.

The manufacturers will give full technical advice and this is worth having as better adhesion and performance can often be obtained by using a specialised primer. The smell of some compounds is nauseating so have good ventilation. Also have gloves and a plentiful supply of Arbo Cleaning Solvent Type 13 for the rubbers as they really are tenacious.

Glass Reinforced Plastic Hulls

Faults that require attention in GRP hulls are caused by original construction faults and lack of quality control. The resins used in GRP construction are technically highly developed – a slipshod craftsman can make technical errors. For example, the mixing of polymers may not be done thoroughly, and the correct working temperature and humidities may not be observed. At this construction stage either a really first-class hull is made – or one that is inferior and which will need a great deal of attention later in its life. Some hulls may actually contain, for cost reasons, inferior materials which give a good first impression but soon develop serious faults. Overloaded and wrong type resin fillers cut down the cost of moulding but signs of failure soon begin to show on the surface. Resins where the polymers have had excessive styrene added to extend them or to make them usable in a cold workshop lead to undercure which later develops into the dreaded boat-pox. This problem develops below the waterline where osmotic action leaches out the free residues which have been unable to polymerise and there is flaking and blistering. There is no space here to go into the technical reasons for GRP failure, but we must learn to look for it and be able to treat any basic fault that might develop.

GRP presents a hard polished surface which is extremely durable, but damage can be done to it. Fig. 2 shows the most vulnerable areas of GRP craft and suggests protective measures.

Polishing

A first-class polish for GRP serves several functions. The easily renewable surface cuts down the effect of weathering, fends off dirt, fills really minute surface imperfections so that dirt does not lodge in them and gives the proud owner a glossy yacht. Many polishes which give an excellent finish contain silicone waxes, and these are not to be recommended as they are extremely difficult to remove if repairs or painting have to be carried out in the future. The leading paint manufacturers have now made available properly constituted polishes. If these are applied according to the manufacturers' instructions they will make the gel coat last well. A good polish will have a screening agent to filter out U.V. light which attacks gel coat colours.

Burnishing pastes

The car paint trade can offer first-class burnishing pastes which can be used to polish out fine surface blemishes and small scratches. Care must be taken that these are not based on a solvent which will attack the gel coat, or of such coarse grades that they will damage the surface more. Care should be taken not to use them extensively and with excessive pressures because the gel coat is of only limited thickness. They are for

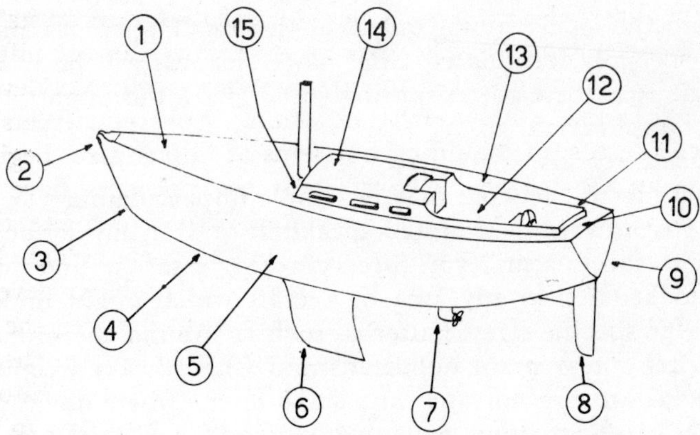

Fig. 2

Area	Cause	Maintenance
1. Foredeck	Anchors, chain and feet	Re-newable paint systems, 'Ferodo' or 'Treadmaster' deck materials.
2. Around fairleads and cleats	Chafe	Mount deck fittings on chafe plates made of wood that can wear away and be re-newed.
3. Stem	Impact from anchors etc	Patch in with epoxy filler and protect with metal bands.
4. Turn of bilge	Floating debris, the tender or when grounding	Wood rubbing strakes on vulnerable areas after patching in.
5. Topsides	Weathering, impact and abrasion from fenders	Patching in gel coat but will eventually need full paint. Use good protective polish to gain maximum life.
6. Keel	From grounding and putting on cradle etc	Stout wood or metal bands after patching in with epoxy system. Dry very thoroughly before working.
7. Round propellers	Most likely in silty operation areas	Use an epoxy putty system to level up damaged areas and renew as necessary.
8. Rudders	Impact damage and from the tender especially	Keep tender from floating up on rising tides. Patch in damaged areas when dry.
9. Transom corners	Particularly liked by harbour walls!	Patching in but nothing compared to really large fenders and care!
10. Aft deck	Especially in 'Med.' mooring to quay	First class deck material with chafe protection for boarding gangway.
11. Coamings	Impact damage	Renewable wood coamings—just cappings, will be best after patching in.
12. Cockpit floors	Foot wear	Painting followed by use of either teak or plastic gratings.
13. Boarding area	Foot wear and impact damage	Non-slip mats are sometimes practical but easily renewable deck coatings are handy.
14. Near mast	From foot wear	Again, non-slip deck paints or areas of deck tread are needed.
15. Corners	Impact and chafe from buckets, rope and feet	Patching in but re-newable wood strip can be preferable for long term protection. Do not lead rope across corners.

severe and local staining only. For cleaning large areas, one of the specially formulated GRP paste cleaners will be in line. Again, use these pastes sparingly and give a thorough waxing after application.

Gel-coat repairs

Cracks in the gel coat may be simple impact damage or very serious outward signs of structural failure. If in any doubt, it is wise to call in a surveyor. Stress cracking is serious and should be looked for in any area of a craft which might undergo regular specific stress patterns, such as around the propeller brackets, near main bulkheads and where heavy weights in general are concentrated in a small area - where davits meet decks or self-steering gears overhang and are fitted onto the transom. Such cracks must be dealt with at a yard as they are more than cosmetic, calling for rebuilding and strengthening. Surface cracks are much more likely to be of a simple nature which we can comfortably deal with.

In the USA, commercial houses have already developed neat aerosol spray kits which have a cunningly engineered means of mixing the catalyst with the coloured resin base. In Europe we can usually obtain the two-part gel coat resins from the hull moulder and do a hand painted repair. Both methods are extremely effective if carried out correctly.

1. Use a household detergent in water to clean off dirt and allow to dry thoroughly. Grease and oil can be removed with a degreasing solvent marketed by 'Little Ship'. Chemical cleansing can then be carried out with Acetone, but beware of inhaling fumes and NEVER allow it to lie in puddles as it destroys GRP if left. Do not allow it to run over gel coats; just give a quick wipe to the damaged area only. Bad cracks may need to be cut back deeper with a rotary sanding disc or small grinder, but great care is needed to ensure the depth of cut is really minimised. The edges can be cleaned back with a coarse grit paper to remove any flaking.

2. Clean off deep abrasions after sanding with a dry clean brush. Use a solventless filler from the epoxy family for deep cracks; on minor abrasions the gel coat can be directly applied. Filler is left lower than the substrata surface to allow a thick gel coat to be applied on top with enough depth to allow it to be rubbed down and not reveal the underlying filler.

3. Mix gel coat parts thoroughly but don't mix in air bubbles. Lay the mix into the crack with a putty knife, leaving it slightly proud of the surrounding surface. I have made successful repairs with shallow cracks using gel coat only and a small spatula made of old vinyl flooring, used as a 'squeegee' to drag a gel coat over the crack.
4. Use either cellophane Sellotaped down or polyvinyl alcohol to seal down the patched area. The smoother the cellophane is pressed down the more perfect the finished surface will be.
5. If the amount of gel coat has been well judged the patch will require next to no sanding down and after the cellophane or PVA has been removed/washed off, wet and dry paper 400 grade followed by 600 used wet will give you a surface ready for a final polishing with a fine cutting compound.

Gel-coat blistering (Osmosis)

The cause already briefly referred to should really be avoided! New yachts and old, if in sound condition, should be thoroughly dried out. New craft should have traces of mould release agent removed. Old craft with anti-fouling on must have this removed till a sound substrata is reached. Although sanding the gel coat is to be recommended and should be carried out on both old anti-fouled surfaces and new gel coats, it *must be done very carefully*: damage will be serious if the gel coat is removed as far as the glass reinforcing! In cases of bad blistering, the gel coat will probably have been damaged to the depth of the reinforcing and this substrata may well be heavily permeated with water. Further ingress of water must be stopped and each damaged patch dried out. This is better done under cover with good heating available. If any trace of water is left under the repair it will create vapour pressure which will cause further trouble. Using a hair-dryer may sound a tedious way of finalising the drying, but if you have tasted serious trouble once you must be prepared to put an end to it. After cleaning and drying, follow these procedures.

1. Use a really sharp chisel to cut back to the sound gel coat around each blister. Keep a sharpening stone to hand for the chisel as it will soon blunt. Do not hit the chisel as blows will crack the gel coat further. Paring and scratching only!
2. Fill all blister holes with an epoxy solventless stopper.
3. Abrade stopper to give mechanical key.

4. Treat the whole of the bottom of the craft with epoxy priming system. I favour epoxy coatings as they are superior in water and abrasion resistance to any other coating and it is this waterproofing that is really needed to protect the boat from blistering. 'Little Ship' red and white epoxy primers are ideal provided the instructions for application are followed exactly. The red epoxy primer can be alternated with white to ensure no 'holidays' are left in successive coatings. I give three coats below the waterline followed directly with the anti-fouling.

An alternative method is to follow up to stage three in preparation and then use a two-can polyurethane painting system. In repairs above the waterline the polyurethane system is much to be preferred, as a finish akin to the original gel coat can, with expertise, be achieved. This high-performance system is not as good as the epoxy one below the waterline, especially for craft used in fresh water. Superlative finishes can be achieved in re-finishing GRP craft with airless spray equipment, but at the present time we are limited to using conventional paint systems with this as the two-can polyurethanes are unsuitable. The electric airless spray is of interest because it is comparatively inexpensive, being a single self-contained unit. Its spray fan is narrower than other spray types and thus it is easier to control the hand held unit.

Steel Yachts

Small steel craft are not made of hefty plating so it is vital to keep corrosion at bay. Be assured, you will never paint over rust and make it last. Wire brushing, though useful to remove loose rust, never, even with a power tool, digs the rust out of the millions of small pits in the metal. Abrasive discing with a power tool is more effective but still limited in removing pitting. The professional can use needle guns and shot blasting which, when well done, is excellent. For us, though, the best method is to wire brush or disc and then use a rust-neutralising phosphoric acid-based proprietry product which will eat into those offending pits. 'Jenolite' and I.C.I. 'Deoxidine 125' are products of this type. Details of Jenolite can be had from the Jenolite Division of Duckham Oils. We are more fortunate now in having the high-performance paint systems and without doubt these are the ones to use on steel.

Aluminium

This is a wonderful material for construction so long as corrosion problems are fully understood and cathodic protection is looked after. It is used not only for hulls but in outdrive casting, outboard motors, window ports and deck fittings, to say nothing of aluminium spars (which are dealt with in the next chapter). Remember its one great enemy is copper, so anti-fouling containing that must never be used on motor castings and hulls. Treating old paint coatings is a matter of brushing down thoroughly with a stainless steel brush then using an etch primer only over any areas of bare metal exposed. This should be followed by one of the high-performance paint systems and then, for under water, an anti-fouling that is guaranteed compatible with aluminium.

Aluminium hull repairs

Most damage to aluminium hulls will be dents. Small ones can be hammered out by making light blows in a circular movement working round from the outside of the dent to the middle, using a backing pad. Larger dents are really the province of the professional for they not only need hammering but heating. The heating is a specialised job as it needs exact control by means of temperature indicating crayons. An area is marked round the outside of the dent with a 400°F (204°C) crayon and the middle with a couple of 500°F (260°C) concentric marks. Heat is applied until the crayon marks start to melt and then immediately withdrawn and hammering started. Continued application of heat may be required and when the result is satisfactory the area is sprayed with water – not the whole plate.

Small dents respond excellently to epoxy resin putties and in fact patches may be applied by this means. Normally, however, patching would require the damaged section to be cut out and a patch matching the area of aluminium removed riveted in with a doubler plate at the back. Fatigue crack in plates must always have holes drilled at the end of the crack to relieve stress before patching. Loose rivets are readily tightened by cold hammering with a back-up hammer held against the opposite end. An epoxy resin adhesive round the old rivet will ensure watertightness.

Keels, Bilge Keels and Centre Boards

Lead for keels is now unfortunately a thing of the past, for this passive metal was almost perfect for the job it had to perform. Corrosion is of course the major enemy again, and even the perfect lead keel had the problem of corrosion in the keel bolts which held it in place. Today, iron has replaced lead.

The cast-iron keel is bolted in place like the lead ones were. Iron below the waterline will corrode badly and certainly should be maintained with an epoxy high-performance paint system. Keel bolts should be drawn every third year for visual inspection. If serious signs of corrosion are showing, superior quality bolts should be substituted and inspected annually to ensure they really are functioning correctly; they can be X-rayed but this is a costly business. One must accept that the bolts are in the most highly corrosive situation of any on a yacht. It is not the direct contact with sea-water so much as the shielding attack they go through, positioned as they are in the thickness of the keel, its mastic sealing and the thickness of the hull. It is at the junction of hull and keel that maximum stress occurs in the bolt and I am quite certain this plays some part in helping to destroy the metal. Iron keels are sometimes used on aluminium yachts and to prevent interaction of the two metals an isolating gasket is used. Provided the keel bolts are sheathed with a sealing and electrically inert compound all will be well. It is true that aluminium and steel have a small potential difference on the galvanic scale, but extreme care is still needed when protective coatings fail (paint scraped off when grounding) and, say, a relatively large area of bilge keel steel is in close proximity to a small scraped area of the aluminium hull. The treatment of steel to maintain it has already been referred to earlier in the chapter.

Whilst the centre board enables a boat to negotiate shallow creeks, it is the very devil to maintain. Small stones and mud jam it up, abrading the inaccessible surfaces. Where centre boarders ground on the tides it is helpful if the board is left protruding just a few inches so that it moves slightly to dislodge mud on each tide. Without access for a brush the yachtsman can fabricate some cunningly shaped painting devices from lengths of wire and synthetic plastic sponges. Do check that the sponge does not disintegrate with the solvents in the paint system you are using and that your better-half is not working underneath as you slosh paint down the centre board. A plastic sheet below will minimise the mess on the ground.

Quite a number of yachts now have complex winding methods for the lowering and raising of the board. Like so many small mechanical items, this one is definitely linked with the yacht's safety so must have special attention paid to it. All wire cables should be regularly inspected. This is often a case of 'easier said than done' and will thus demand extra willpower. Look for broken wire strands, distorted thimbles and signs of corrosion. Keep drive gears well lubricated with a water repellent grease. Try to keep grease to a minimum so that it does not contaminate surfaces you will later have to paint.

Chapter 5
MAST, RIGGING AND SAILS

The wind may be free but I'm blessed if the rest of the gear is. The total cost may be as much - or a deal more than - the iron topsail below, so just as much effort should be put into maintenance. When surveying a boatyard in winter it would appear that this is not understood by most yachtsmen, for we see forests of masts with rigging flogging away in the winter winds. It is foolish to assume that modern materials such as aluminium, stainless steel and synthetic ropes have properties which enable them to withstand the elements without corrosion or rotting and that it is a waste of time and money to lay up the mast. Materials today are better at standing up to the elements than they used to be - but they are still less than perfect. Aluminium will corrode where the protective anodising has been damaged; stainless steel and aluminium have a fatigue life; synthetic ropes will chafe and deteriorate with weathering. A mast standing up needlessly to a winter gale will have its life shortened. Laying up is a much better investment, as the mast and rigging will then be in tip-top condition if you meet a gale later at sea. Besides, when the mast is laid up, it is the only time a really thorough inspection (see Fig. 3) can be made and maintenance carried out.

Unstepping masts needs considerable skill in planning and execution. A careful estimation of your own ability and the amount of help available will dictate if you are to call in the profesionals or do the job yourself. The following points should be considered.

1. Navigation lights - check bulbs, wiring & spring contacts.
2. Mast head instruments-wiring.
3. Internal sheaves must run freely. No wear on pins or sheaves.
4. Spreader sockets - fatigue cracks, fastener failure.
5. Radar reflector rigged correctly in "catch rain" position. Check accuracy of reflecting surfaces.
6. Provide chafe protection on standing rigging.
7. Shroud tangs - no enlargement of fastener hole in mast section.
8. Track - clean and check for any deformation.
9. Gooseneck / roller reefing gear - clean & service mechanical parts.
10. Service halliard winches.
11. Check mounting plate or gaskets on through deck masts.
12. Rigging fittings free from fatigue distortion must be cleaned. Split pins or monel wire mousing must be taped over when re-rigging to prevent sail damage.
13. Chain plate & deck plates free from fatigue, fasteners good & water-tight.
14. Boom parts are serviced like mast parts.
15. Check foresail and genoa track, fasteners, sliders. Track is very vulnerable to impact damage.
16. Check bottlescrews for elongation (fatigue). Forestay bottlescrews should always have toggles fitted.

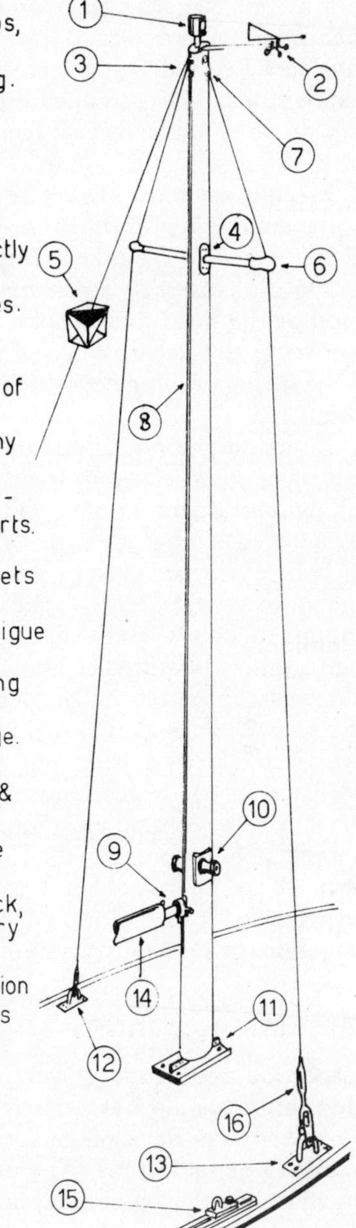

Fig. 3. Mast Care

1. Masts of over 25 feet or more require special equipment. Shearlegs, strops and tackles are costly to set up safely and will have to be stored for future use. Small masts can easily be manhandled. Masts stepped on deck are a modern benefit as they do not require several feet of vertical lift before clearing the deckhouse.
2. Precautions must always be taken on decks and cabin tops to prevent the foot of the mast scraping and to allow the thrust of its weight to be taken. Support to a cabin roof can be arranged by inserting a post held in position by a deck plate of wood at the head and a plate plus wedges at the foot. Don't overwedge to force up the roof and secure a post with lanyards as the spring of some decks is sufficient to allow even wedges to shift.
3. Be as punctilious about the quality of the tackles, blocks and ropes you use as you would be about the actual rigging. A falling mast might damage you or the crew in a serious way, to say nothing of what it will do to itself and the boat.
4. Before anyone gets to work prepare all shackles, bottle screws, clevis pins, etc. so that they are untaped and free to be undone quickly when the need arises.

Masts may be stored either as a ridge pole over the length of the yacht supported on proper leather-lined scissor crutches, chocks or boom gallows, or in a shed. I would advise that the shed is by far the best, but just as much exact support is needed over the whole length of the mast to keep it perfectly straight – yes, even an aluminium one. Some yachtsmen prefer a single pole support for the ridge guyed with four lanyards to deck cleats or stanchion bases. The bottom of all devices giving support to a winter cover will need covering in foam to stop damage to the surfaces they rest on.

Mast Maintenance

Inspection and washing over is the first step. Both wood and aluminium should have salt removed, then each fitting must be looked over for signs of fatigue (Fig. 3 indicates the main points to be looked at). Any minute cracks in any metal part may just be the start of a serious failure.

A simple visual test for cracks in loose fittings can be made by first mechanically polishing, then heating the fitting in a clean flame until it begins to get too hot to hold, when it is transferred to pliers to gain just a little extra heat. Then immerse it in a mixture of light oil and paraffin (one part oil to three parts paraffin) for fifteen minutes. Next wipe the suspect fitting over with a mixture of methyl alcohol/zinc oxide, and you will see cracks and scratches shown up as dark lines as the film dries. After repolishing out scratches the test is redone and a crack will reappear in the same position.

Loose rivets, worn sheaves, distorted shackles or bent rigging screws all call for repairs or replacement.

Cleaning and painting

Wooden masts are subject to rot. Look especially under mast bands where wood has been compressed, damaging the protective finish, where fastenings enter the wood and at the foot. For this reason I never like to see a mast painted, as varnish allows the darkening of the wood to show through and this is a good indication that things are beginning to go wrong. To varnish a mast or spar well, all fittings need to be stripped off. The mast can then be scraped down using small oblongs of newly-cut glass (wear leather gloves to stop the raw edge cutting you). As the glass goes blunt, cut another thin strip off it and you have the best paint scraper there is available. Sand down thoroughly before treating the newly-exposed wood with a clear preservative. Then proceed in the normal way.

Aluminium (not anodised) will corrode by forming rough white powdery deposits. On a mast, this roughening will play havoc with sails and running rigging, chafing them to an early demise. Rubbing a spar down with stainless steel wire wool and wax polishing will do for a season or two, but by far the best remedy is to paint with a high-performance system, preferably an epoxy which will provide a smooth surface and stand up to really hard wear. First degrease the surface, follow with an aluminium etch primer, then the paint system you have chosen.

Anodising aluminium gives it a protective coat that will resist corrosion for years provided scratching and abrasion are avoided. Never use an abrasive on it. All that is required is a wash down and wax polish at laying-up time. Never lash stainless steel rigging to spars at laying-up time as in damp conditions this can promote galvanic corrosion between dissimilar metals. Slight dents in aluminium masts may be acceptable but deeper dents should receive the attention of the professional spar maker.

Addition of fittings to aluminium spars needs care but can be done by the handyman. Lightly loaded fittings can be held by means of stainless steel self-tapping screws. Heavily loaded fittings must be through-bolted into fixed pads on the mast. Alternatively, use blind rivets such as 'Gesipa', brand marketed by Goad's. These rivets are available in either aluminium head with stainless steel mandrel or as all stainless steel. Avoid drilling holes in line round a spar as these will weaken it. Provided holes are not less than ¾in (19mm) apart in a vertical line they do not reduce strength more than a single hole.

The mast head and spreaders take the main stress from the shrouds and could be the places where fatigue will show. Inspect anemometer and wind direction gear to make sure it is weathering well.

Internal cables which serve mast head instruments and navigation lights must be inspected for chafe and to see that connectors are in good order. Attach a stout drawstring to the cable being removed for inspection or renewal; the cable is then simply redrawn up the mast to pull it back into position.

Standing Rigging

This may be made up of either galvanised or stainless steel wire rope, usually 1 × 19 or 7 × 7. The fewer the wires the higher the breaking load for a given diameter, and the lower both stretch and price. However, 1 × 19 is not for hand splicing. Galvanised wire will corrode and rust staining and snags can give a bloody reminder that the time has come for replacement. Never run fingers over them without the protection of a strong cloth. Stainless steel rigging is cleaned by washing down. It too can snag, but this is more likely to be a fatigue failure sign rather than internal corrosion as it is with galvanised wire rope. The place to look for trouble is not so much in the rope as in the terminals at either end of it. The weakest place is always the end fitting or splices.

Terminals are, if unprofessionally done, the weak link and because the job is done by machine it takes a real professional to know that it has been done correctly. They come in a variety of types—eyes, forks and studs—and are put on by

Mechanical roll or rotary hammer, which rolls the body of the terminal into the strands of wire rope. It cannot be removed once done but it is comforting to know that the aircraft industry, which has such high safety standards, approves this method. Look for fatigue where the wire enters the terminal body.

Hand fitted terminals, of which 'Norseman' are pre-eminent in the world, are well up to the highest standards of safety if properly done and they have the advantage that expensive machinery is not required. The ability to work on site will attract most yachtsmen.

Talurit splicing requires a professional with a machine and can be used on both stainless and galvanised wire so long as the former uses the copper ferrule and the galvanised an alloy one.

Bottlescrews should be taken apart if they are of the closed barrel type as this is where water can lodge and corrosion begin. Units which are machined from Type 316 stainless steel have amazing ductile properties and are able to withstand 50 per cent elongation before they break. I do not suggest you should load your rigging to try this out, but you can compare a new and an old unit to see if indeed elongation of a small percentage is taking place so that strain is detected before failure occurs. Forestay bottlescrews should always have a toggle fitted to take care of the athwartship thrust of the genoa.

Thimbles should always be made of material which does not allow them to distort when loaded.

Shackles are often used in rigging but are not recommended. Proper toggles are the correct thing. However, check any shackles for wear on the pin and always see they are moused when re-rigging.

Track and fittings

The smooth operation of sail hoisting and lowering, of main sheet adjustment and foresail and genoa sliders all depends on the track being kept clean and free of mechanical damage which prevents the movement of sail slide or fittings. Both internal and external track should be cleaned first with water and then with a toothbrush and LPS aerosol spray. Spinnaker pole tracks are the most likely place to find damage, especially if you are unfortunate enough to have bronze sliders which have a nasty habit of digging into the track and cutting away its edges. Repair the track or have it renewed and change over to the sliders with nylon inserts that will fray neither the edge of the track nor the temper of the crew. Apart from the crew, anything on the foredeck that moves by sliding, pivoting or snapping shut must be winterised by washing and treating to a shot of LPS.

Winches for halyards and sheets vary enormously in their design from the simple plain bearing models for small craft to the most frightfully expensive 'coffee-grinders' used on ocean racers. They have a hard life, being exposed to the elements on deck and to severe usage. They therefore demand proper mechanical maintenance if they are to function properly. Since it is impossible to list every available yacht winch made that needs servicing, I would heartily recommend any yachtsman to go direct to the maker of his particular set of winches and buy the full service manual from them. I was extremely impressed by the service manuals available from Barlow and Lewmar, which give information about spares and service notes down to the very last detail. The correct greases which stand up to sea-water and light oil lubricants for lighter moving parts such as ratchets must be observed.

Routine servicing on a monthly basis is recommended throughout the season when ratchets, pawls and their associated springs can be oiled and bearings greased. At the end of the season it is recommended that a full service is carried out. By far the best way of doing this is to remove the whole winch from the boat and take it to a comfortable workshop where all the small pieces will not get lost. Unfortunately, boats are usually built so that this is almost impossible, so the next best thing is carefully to dismantle all the parts and take these home for cleaning and then bring them back to the boat to be built up, following the instructions in a manual. (Fig. 4 shows one of the Lewmar range of winches with typical maintenance instructions and parts list.) One could wish that all manufacturers of mechanical

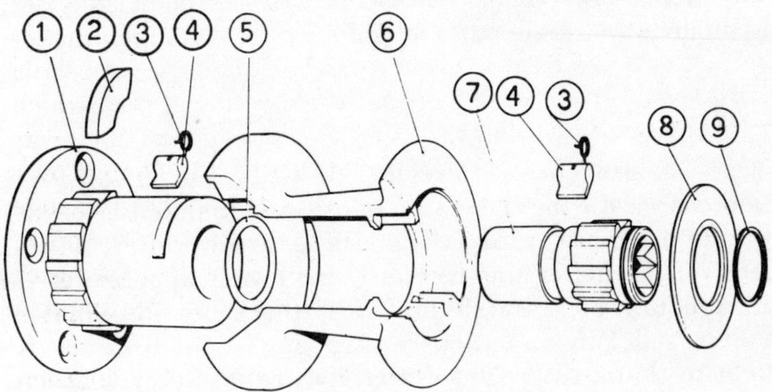

Lewmar Single Speed Winches Nos. 6 & 7.

Maintenance
A Remove circlip (9) using a small screwdriver or knife blade. Use a spiral motion to remove from groove.
B Lift drum (6) and cover plate (8) from centre stem (1).
C Remove cover plate (8) from drum (6).

The winch is now ready for routine monthly maintenance.

D Clean off excess grease and salt deposits from bearing surface of drum (6) and centre stem (1).
E Check free operation of pawls (4) in upper and lower parts of drum (6).
F Check free rotation of spindle (7) in centre stem (1).
G If satisfactory proceed with routine maintenance. If not continue with FULL SERVICE PROCEDURE.
H Lightly grease the bore of the drum (6) and the bearing surface of centre stem (1).
I Lightly oil the pawls.
J Lightly oil the centre spindle (7).
K Re-assemble drum (6) to centre stem (1) by introducing drum over centre spindle and turning clock-wise to engage lower pawls. Hold upper pawls out with fingers to finally lower drum into position.
L Rotate drum (6) to check freedom of pawl movement and correct engagement. Rotate spindle (1) to check complete engagement of top pawls.
M Replace top cap.
N Replace circlip (9) by entering one end into groove and winding circlip into position.
O Using handle check free operation of winch and correct engagement of pawls.

Full Annual Service
P Dismantle as per steps A - C.
Q Remove four pawls (4) and pawl springs (3) from the winch drum (6).
R Remove spindle retaining key (2) from centre stem (1) with small screwdriver or knife blade.
S Remove spindle (7) and washer (5) from centre stem (1).
T Carefully wash drum, centre stem, spindle washer, pawls springs and spindle key.
U Lightly grease drum bore, centre stem bearing area, spindle.
V Assemble spindle (7) to centre stem (1) with washer (5) in position. Replace spindle retaining key (2).
W Replace four pawls (4) and four springs (3) in drum, and lightly oil.
X Complete reassembly and testing as points K - O.
Y If winch fails to perform correctly re-check servicing technique or contact your nearest Lewmar service point.

Parts list

No. 6

Item Number	Part Number	Description	No of
1	15006001	Centre Stem	1
2	15006005	Key	1
3	1260/7	Pawl Spring	4
4	1260/8	Pawl	4
5	15006004	Washer	1
6	15006102 15006202	Drum, Bronze Drum, Alloy	1
7	15006003	Spindle	1
8	15006006	Top Cap	1
9	B 2075	Circlip	1

No. 7

Item Number	Part Number	Description	No of
1	15007001	Centre Stem	1
2	15010005	Key	1
3	1260/7	Pawl Spring	4
4	1260/8	Pawl	4
5	15006004	Washer	1
6	15008102 15008202	Drum, Bronze Drum, Alloy	1
7	15006003	Spindle	1
8	15006006	Top Cap	1
9	B2075	Circlip	1

Fig.4. Sample Winch Maintenance.

components for yachts provided such explicit servicing instructions and spare parts service.

Sails

Their maintenance is really divided into two parts: maintenance during the season in use, and maintenance when sails are not in use, especially out of season in winter. Both of these will be better understood if the owner appreciates the vast amount of research and skill that goes into making modern sailcloth and then constructing a sail from it. We ought to thank the racing fraternity, for it is they who have constantly badgered sailcloth makers and the sailmakers to give them products that will drive the sailing yacht to as near perfection as technology allows. We don't all race, but we may always have extra peace of mind if we are able to think that the sails will give us maximum drive off a lee shore or even get us into port in time to keep appointments that we would really far rather forget about. Fig. 5 shows the main points in sail maintenance.

Sail materials

These should be identified so that safe treatments can be given. Nylon, Dacron or Terylene are all modern synthetic fibres which may be used in sail-making. The synthetic threads are first doubled or folded together to create a yarn, the yarn is then 'set' by various processes to deaden it ready for creeling, where it is made up by hand into several hundred packages ready for beaming; this is the process for creating the warp beam. The warp threads are then sized to bind each one together and act as a lubricant during the weaving process; this prevents fraying of the threads. The weaving is done on looms which have as much attention paid to their 'tuning' (which gets the tensions of warp and weft to a perfection) as the successful racing yachtsman gives to tuning his yacht. The final process is to 'finish' the cloth, sometimes with calendering (thermal shrinkage of the fabric) or by much guarded chemical impregnation or resinous materials.

Damage is done to sails because we interfere with the weave of the cloth or destroy the special finishes given. The following sail cleaning information is in good faith, but no responsibility

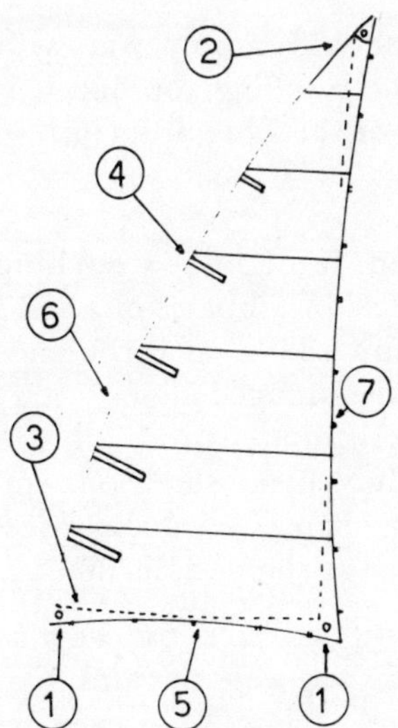

1. Check tack and clew eyes.
2. Headboard - wear from halyard shackle and chafe.
3. Badly stretched sails can be re-cut-with sailmakers advice.
4. Check batten pockets.
5. Check stitching on foot.
6. Check leach stitching. Look for chafe damage from rigging.
7. Check slides and hanks or the cloth and stitching around the luff rope.

SAIL INSPECTION

BOOM COVERS

8. Must be water and U.V. light proof
9. Lacing does not crush the flaked down sail like shock cords.
10. Lacing must be tight around mast.

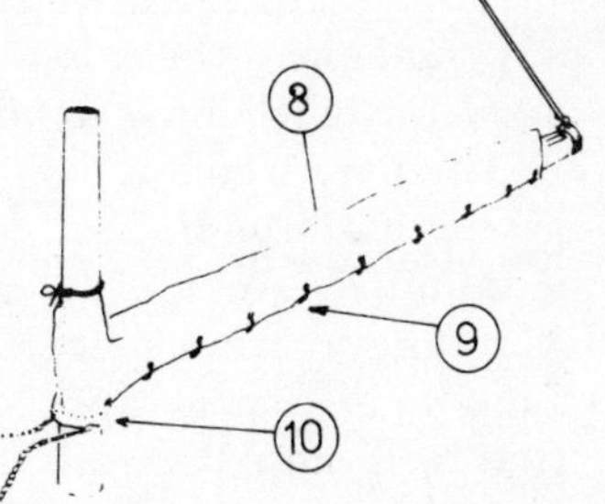

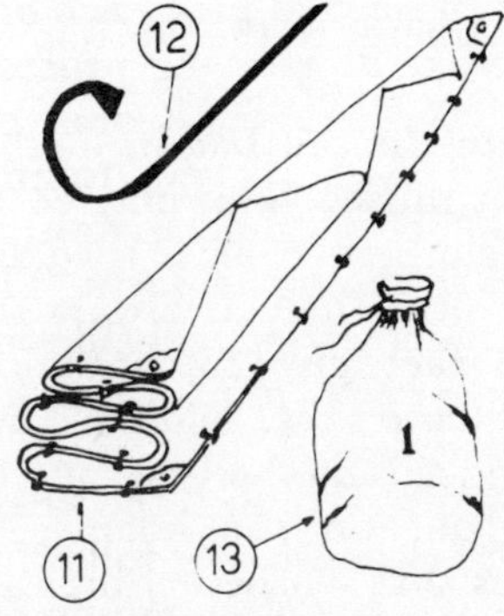

STOWING

11. Flake down light sails.
12. Roll from foot to headboard
13. Be generous with size of sail bags. Do not crush with anchors! Clean and dry sails before storing.

Fig.5. Sail Care

can be accepted. Your sail-maker should supply you with details of the exact type of material he is selling you and it is then up to you to contact the makers of the fibre and cloth to give you specific instructions.

Care during use

Stretching in any form is a cardinal sin. It might be stretching caused by hauling down on that weakest of all parts of a sail – the leech – so that it looks like an animated 'Z' as turbulence destroys the smooth flow of air from its damaged edge. It may be stretching caused by an indiscriminate prod with a spinnaker pole or where the sail has been slept on and stretched over a sharp projection on deck. Any local stress loading on the delicate fibres will damage them. Sails that are not taken down when the wind pipes up to a Force they were never designed to accommodate will stretch and never regain their original shape. This means their performance will never be the same. Re-cutting may alleviate damage but cannot achieve a full cure to an over-driven sail.

Chafe, a perpetual enemy because synthetic fibre materials do not allow the delicate stitching to bed down into the material. It lies exposed on the surface and chafe against various parts of the rigging cuts it through. Fig. 3 gives some indication of methods of minimising chafe by employing various types of fixed gadgets, ranging from split tennis balls, empty washing-up liquid containers, plastic tapes, old mop heads and indeed anything that will stop the sails from rubbing on rigging booms or masts. In the end, though, the prevention of chafe depends on the skipper keeping an eye on places where chafe is liable to occur so that constant adjustments to the positioning of running rigging minimises it.

Stowing so often means stuffing into the sail bag in double quick time so that not a pint shall be missed! This may be all right with a light and soft nylon cloth such as is used for spinnakers, but for heavier filled cloths there is always the danger of creasing which will in fact give minute local stretching to the woven fibres. For loose sails, folding down and rolling is to be recommended and this method can also be applied where mainsails are left out on the boom. An important point to remember here is that synthetic fibres are subject to a chemical decay in ultra-violet light. This is a good reason for always providing a really good boom cover. Though lacing a boom cover to give full protection takes time, I am greatly in favour of this method as a low tension can be given so that local creasing is avoided. Shock cords tend to crush local areas, and I never like shock cords with stainless steel hooks near the metal boom in case they scratch the anodised surface. The sail cover will also keep off seagull guano and a bit of the pollution that seems to be encroaching on the fresh air near parts of our coasts.

Washing during the season is to be encouraged, since it will free the cloth of salt and dirt picked up. Again, this is a council of perfection as the average yachtsman away from marina berth will not have a plentiful supply of fresh water on hand to do the job. A sail that has been hosed down should be hoisted by the tack and the head secured at deck level to dry out, making sure it does not catch obstructions as it blows in the wind to leeward. A sail can be washed at home on long grass, but do be sure the area is clean first and that the sail is not left lying there for long. I remember doing just that and the worms, being thankful that I had provided such a massive area of shade, proceeded to make worm casts under it and the result was as if the sail had been dragged through deep mud! Don't wash on hard surfaces such as concrete as this will chafe stitching. A way out is to buy builders' polythene sheeting, which is quite inexpensive, and use this over otherwise unsuitable surfaces to protect the sails. It is also good for protecting bathroom floors from floods as sails are transferred from there to drying grounds.

Thorough washing at the end of the season is vital and if sails are too big for the owner to handle they should go away for professional treatment. The proprietary liquid detergents which are known as soapless detergents are safe on all sail fabrics if used at hand temperature - about 50°C for white or 40°C for coloured cloths. Enamel or plastic baths (so long as metal fittings don't scratch them) and porcelain (pottery) sinks are best for the job; metal ones, except stainless steel, must be avoided. Modern detergent powders are usually alkaline and although it is perfectly all right to use them if really thorough rinsing is given, Terylene can be damaged in the long run if the rinsing is neglected.

Terylene sails that are badly soiled may be steeped overnight in cold water containing 1lb per gallon (100g per litre) of metasilicate. After this soak, drain the solution away and hand wash in warm water. Metal parts must be kept out of this solution, especially galvanised luff wires which will be attacked.

Coloured sails must only be treated with the gentlest of washing treatments and only professional cleaning services used for stubborn marks.

Sails must be hung out to dry with their weight supported by the luff over its whole length.

Removal of stains

This is best done at the time they occur. Solvents used in cleaning compounds can be dangerous, being inflammable and/or poisonous, so *read the instructions and adhere to them.*

Blood. Though Nelson painted his gun decks red so that his sailors would not be put off by the sight of blood swilling about, this is no excuse for the skipper to buy red sails to show his concern for foredeck crew! Their blood can easily be removed from sails by washing immediately in a solution of half a cupful of ammonia in a gallon (4L) of water. Residual stains may be further treated with a one per cent solution of pepsin in water acidified with a few drops of dilute hydrochloric acid. Allow this to stand on the stain for thirty minutes then rinse thoroughly. Do not treat nylon with this solution.

Mildew is a more likely stain than blood and is caused through poor storage conditions. Brush the sail to remove surface mould growth then soak the mildewed area for two hours in a mixture of ten parts water to one of proprietary Domestos or a sodium hypochlorite solution with one per cent available chlorine. Wash the sail thoroughly and repeat the bleach process if staining is still bad, followed by another washing. The chlorine smell can be removed by immersion of the sail in a one per cent solution of sodium thiosulphate (photographers' hypo) followed by another rinse.

Grease, oil and waxes can be removed by using proprietary stain removers based on trichloroethylene, which is a dangerous material to have around the confined spaces of a boat. Far better to use a hand-cleansing gel such as Duckham's Palmit, which no doubt the engineer already has aboard for his own hands. The painter might also have Polyclens aboard and this can be used by brushing well into the fabric like Palmit, leaving for fifteen minutes then washing out.

Metallic stains may be left as the residue from oil stains or directly from verdigris from copper and bronze fittings, or rust staining from deteriorating galvanised wires. The solutions suggested above will remove staining from cloth but they will also attack metal fittings, galvanising or copper, so they must never be used in contact with them. Rust marks are best removed with a solution made up by dissolving 1oz (25g) oxalic acid in 1 pint (575ml) hot water (poisonous). This is not recommended for nylon. Alternatively, soak the stain for ten minutes in a warm solution of 2 per cent hydrochloric acid then wash off thoroughly; again this is not recommended for nylon and contact with metal parts must be avoided at all costs.

Pitch and tar. White spirit is the most likely and safe solvent to be handy in the bosun's locker. Proprietary solvents based on trichloroethylene may be used but one must be careful not to spread staining by always working from the outside of the damage towards the centre. It is also advisable to blot up excess dirty solvent to prevent that spreading.

Paint and varnish may be removed with white spirit if this is done immediately, but equal parts of acetone and amyl acetate swabbed onto the stain after dabbing with trichloroethylene will remove it. Always wash after using these materials and keep acetone and amyl acetate away from GRP surfaces. Strong alkaline compounds as used in paint strippers will damage Terylene.

Storage

Dry, clean storage of sails properly folded and rolled, avoiding sharp creases, will preserve well-cleaned sails in perfect order throughout the winter. The loft in your house could make an excellent 'sail loft', provided it is sealed off from ingress of dirt and birds. I have done just the opposite, however, and found some really fine dry space under the main living area, where I have increased ventilation to provide first-class winter storage.

Chapter 6
THE ENGINE

The days when we looked on a yachtsman as a true expert when he could sail on and off his moorings have long since gone. Nothing could be less seaman-like than to attempt such manoeuvres in today's overcrowded anchorages and marinas. We have all come to be dependant on the 'iron topsail' to look after the safety of manoeuvring and to give us safe passage in the worst of weathers.

The marine engine is one of the most expensive single items aboard so attention to its needs will not only ensure a greater safety factor but will minimise spending hefty sums on righting mechanical faults that could have been avoided if the correct maintenance had been given.

Probably the most important thing is to know your own capabilities and to gain confidence in your knowledge of the engine in your yacht. Merely looking at an engine is not going to damage it. Get to know all the parts of a petrol or diesel engine that you may need to maintain. Fig. 6 shows parts of petrol engines that could need regular attention.

A constant complaint from marine engine manfuacturers is that owners seldom, if ever, bother to read their engine service manuals. These are specially written in a straightforward manner and give all the basic information that is vital if the engine is to be maintained in the condition it deserves. I like to get hold of the professional service manual for any marine engine I have, for even though a number of jobs will be quite beyond me, needing expensive and specialised tools, they give

a much deeper insight into the engine which certainly helps me to give it better treatment and diagnose engine faults when they develop. If you can learn to give a professional mechanic an accurate description of the mechanical symptoms, you are going to save a great deal of time and money. If you simply say, 'The engine won't start', or 'The engine's making a funny noise', you immediately, at best, ensure that the competent mechanic is going to spend extra time finding a more precise diagnosis. At worst, you lay yourself wide open to the shark who will provide a bill which escalates in direct proportion to the yachtsman's own ignorance. With a genuine interest in your own pocket and safety you are not likely to be in such ranks.

Mechanic's Tools

If you do intend working on your engine, make up your mind to be kind to it. Attacking it with a lump hammer, cold chisels instead of screwdrivers and ill-fitting spanners of a past era constitutes a form of cruelty that should be punishable by law! You never save money by purchasing cheap tools; not only are they badly made to low tolerances, but the steel in them is inferior in every way. They will break prematurely or will rust so fast as to be worse than useless. A quality chrome vanadium steel spanner will last a lifetime and will always be a joy to use because it is clean and fits perfectly. The damp, salt atmosphere of a boat is anathema to certain steels - they will start rusting immediately they are put aboard. Some yachtsmen wrap tools in greasy rags to stop rust, but I find that the modern plastic tool box will keep tools in perfect condition if they are given an occasional squirt of one of the proprietary aerosol rust prevention sprays. These sprays are much easier to clean off when the tools are wanted and are less likely therefore to slip whilst being used and dropped into the bilges.

Most USA and British engine manufacturers use AF (American Fine) fastener threads and nuts. Therefore, if you have such an engine, an AF set of spanners is needed. I'm sorry to relate that even at this late date, Whitworth threads are still in evidence. Whitworth is supposed to be a redundant system,

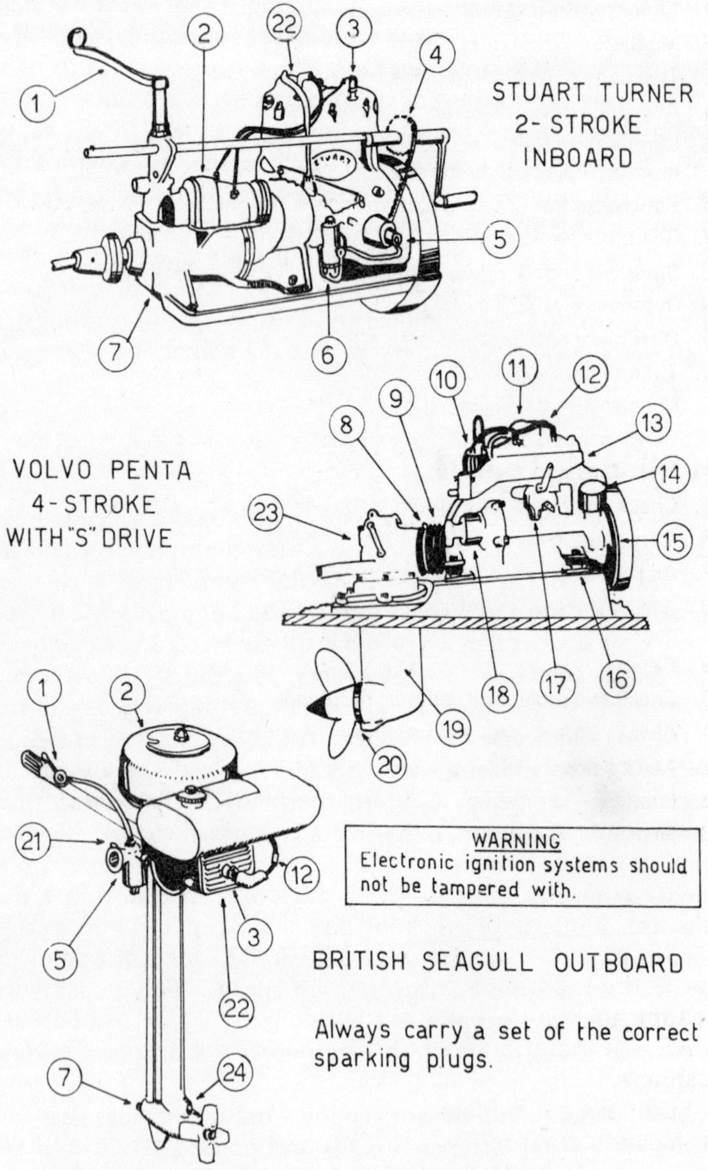

Fig. 6. Points in Petrol Engine (inboard, outdrive and outboard) Maintenance and Winterisation

1. Check and lubricate gear shifts, controls and cables.
2. Magnetos, generators and starter motors must be stored dry.
3. Clean and gap sparking plugs.
4. Any chain drives clean and lubricate.
5. Carburettors fuel lines, fuel pumps and tanks drained for winter. They must be sealed off during storage.
6. Raw water from cooling systems and pumps must be drained down.
7. Gearbox - service oil and check levels. Service filter if any.
8. Outdrives and 'S' drives - check bellows clips *regularly.*
9. Outdrives and 'S' drives - check bellows *regularly.*
10. Distributor and coils serviced.
11. Thermostats checked if running temperatures are wrong.
12. Check all electrical leads, especially H.T. ones.
13. Check sooting on manifolds and cooling injection bends.
14. Main engine oil check levels, winterise and change filter.
15. Check any belt drive and adjust to correct tension. Carry spare.
16. All mountings keep tight and free from oil.
17. Air intakes and flame traps, clean and seal off for winter.
18. Jabsco pumps to be drained down and services on indirect cooled engines and where this type of pump is used on direct systems.
19. Paint and anti-foul outdrive and 'S' drive legs *correctly*.
20. Check and replace all cathodic protection.
21. Always note engine number for security and spares.
22. Any cylinder must be winterised with a drop of oil.
23. Lubricate outdrive and 'S' drive gears correctly. Check seals.
24. Flush out water cooling systems and winterise.

but a wise yachtsman will carry a set of Whitworth spanners. As time goes on, we shall be metricated so even if your engine is AF you may find other fittings needing yet another set of spanners.

European engines use metric threads but never be surprised at the odd variety of threads that turn up aboard a boat. If you have room, a small set of open and ring spanners is preferable to just one type as your main problem with engine servicing is to find room to get spanners onto nuts at all let alone turn them. If you are really ambitious, or just want to save the skin on your knuckles, I would certainly recommend getting a small tool set such as Bedford of Sheffield manufacture. Their 'Allsorts' sets consist of open-ended spanners, ring spanners and sockets with various drives. These small sets are compact enough for the smallest yacht, but for larger nuts you should also carry adjustable wrenches.

Deep-set nuts can often be reached only with a socket on a drive shaft. An 8in or 10in adjustable wrench will serve most purposes, but every yacht should carry one really big wrench. This will serve for the small number of very large nuts that inevitably need attention such as skin fitting nuts, propeller shaft gland nuts and propeller boss nuts. A petrol engine will need the correct size plug spanner.

Stanley Tools Ltd. (UK and USA) make a good range of screwdrivers – and there is nothing like the correct screwdriver for the job. Fiddling around with a wide flared screwdriver when attempting to do up wire connections inside a plug is as infuriating as attempting to tighten up a ½in slotted head bolt with an electrician's screwdriver. Always match the screwdriver to the screw. This will ensure you don't damage surrounding wood or metal and the slot in the screw head is preserved. You will come across a number of Philips and GKN Pozidriv cross head screws. These are a boon as a driver does not easily 'cam out' in them, thus preventing damage that occurs to the slot, especially when screw heads are often in blind areas.

Pliers and an electrician's wire baring and crimping tool make up my basic list. 'Hella' make a small kit of electrical crimp connectors complete with this tool and it's very useful to have a set aboard. A word of warning, though: don't overcrimp the terminals with a too hefty pressure on the tool. You will damage the small conductor wires and fatigue will ensure that the connection soon drops off!

The elaborateness of your final choice of tools will depend on the size of both your yacht and pocket. Apart from a full socket set, my yacht's service kit fits into a plastic box 14 × 10 × 4in (35.5 × 25.5 × 10cm) – not a great deal of space.

If you have now purchased a quality set of tools you can begin to retrieve their cost by getting to work on the engine.

Believe me, at today's rate of pay for the professional mechanic, you will soon do this! Let's look at a graded list of jobs the amateur can competently carry out on the marine engine, starting with petrol motors.

Petrol marine engines

Always clean around parts of the engine before dismantling so that dirt does not fall inside.

Spark plugs

Don't worry at this stage whether your engine is a two- or four-stroke type; both will have a spark plug or, if multi-cylinder, a number of spark plugs. The correct plug spanner will ensure that after removing the high tension electrical leads from the top of the plugs you will be able to remove each plug without damaging the ceramic insulator. A cracked insulator certainly means a new plug, so inspect it carefully. Next look at the inside of the plug. It's amazing the story this can tell, and a plug manufacturer will often let you have a leaflet with diagnostic photographs which tell you exactly what has been happening in the engine's combustion space.

Two-stroke petrol engines are the ones that have oil added to the fuel for their lubrication. Too much oil in the fuel and the combustion in the upper cylinder is incomplete and the excess oil soon oils up the plug. Engine manufacturers and oil companies have worked wonders in recent years to produce reliable two-stroke oils especially for high-performance outboard motors, but even the best seem to get spasms of oiling up. Don't dig at the inside of the plug with an electrician's screwdriver to remove the oily carbon you find there: the inside ceramic insulator will crack if you prod the central electrode. Used carefully, a fine wire brush dipped in petrol will usually do a temporary cleaning job. (Be careful with that petrol!)

Always carry spare plugs so that dirty ones can be professionally cleaned on a machine at your local garage. On plugs with one side electrode, make sure this is the one bent to adjust it to the proper gap. You will need a feeler gauge for this setting and the engine manual will give the correct gap setting. When replacing plugs, do not over-tighten them down and try to use a new seating gasket, especially if the old one is entirely flattened. Discoloured or corroded surfaces where this gasket beds down indicate gas leakage due to insufficient tightening or uneven seatings.

With clean threads, the plug should first be screwed down until it is finger tight. A further half turn with a plug spanner will then ensure the gasket forms a seal but is not over compressed. If you are suffering from radio interference, why not, as a first step in eradicating it, fit an A.C. (General Motors) resistor type spark plug? These greatly reduce radio frequency interference signals, especially in the VHF bands.

Magneto ignition engines (petrol inboard and outboard units)

Although slowly fading from the boating scene, the magneto ignition system is still found on a vast number of small marine engines, both in petrol outboard and petrol inboard two-stroke units. They generate the spark or sparks for ignition without the need for cumbersome batteries. Basically the magneto works in the following manner.

The magneto shaft, permanent magnet and laminated pole shoes form a single assembly known as the rotor. This, supported on ball bearings, revolves between a pair of laminated pole pieces in the stator. These stator pole pieces are bridged by the laminated core of a coil, having a primary winding of relatively few turns of thick wire and a secondary winding of many turns of fine wire. A contact breaker is arranged to interrupt the primary circuit at the instant a spark is required.

The rotor, driven by the engine, produces an alternating field in the iron core of the coil. This field induces alternating voltages in the primary and secondary windings of the coil. Magnetic flux due to current flowing in the primary winding opposes any change in direction of the magnetic field in the coil core, In this way, the field reversals due to the rotating magnets are delayed until the contact breaker opens. At this moment, the restraining influence of the primary winding is removed and the consequent rapid reversal of the magnetic field linked with the coil causes a high voltage to be induced in the secondary winding.

With single-cylinder engines this high voltage is conducted direct to the plug via the high tension cable, but with multi-cylinder units it is taken to a rotating electrode in the cable cover and distributed to each spark plug in turn.

Impulse starter

This consists of two members flexibly coupled by a clock-type spring. One member is secured to the magnetic spindle while the other carries the driving dogs or sprockets. When cranking the engine, the member secured to the spindle is first prevented from turning by a pawl or trip lever. The coupling spring is therefore wound up until a projection on the driving member trips the pawl. The magnetic rotor is then rapidly accelerated through the sparking position, thus increasing its intensity and, because of the mechanical geometry, automatically retarding the spark which we need for a good easy start. The impulse starter can then relieve some of the frantic cranking speed that was often required on engines not equipped with this refinement. Fig. 7 shows the basic parts of two commonly found magneto ignition systems.

Basic servicing and maintenance may be summarised as follows.

1. Always keep the magneto dry and clean both inside and out. Damp in dust and dirt will allow current leakage. Damp will gradually break down the electrical windings.

2. The magneto is a timed unit. The points must make and break at a precise instant determined by the particular engine manufacturer. When removing a magneto from an engine, mark both the magneto and the engine coupling to eliminate error when re-installing. Some engine manufacturers already make timing marks on their units, so know about these or look for them.

3. Replacement and setting of breaker points is the main servicing job and spare sets of points and the correct condenser should be carried. Lucas have long since given up the manufacture of magnetos although their 'SR' models may still be found giving good service. Contact them direct to see if spares are still available. The Wipac Group produce 'Wipac' or 'Wico' magnetos for a considerable range of marine engines including Stuart Turner, Britt, British Anzani, Coventry

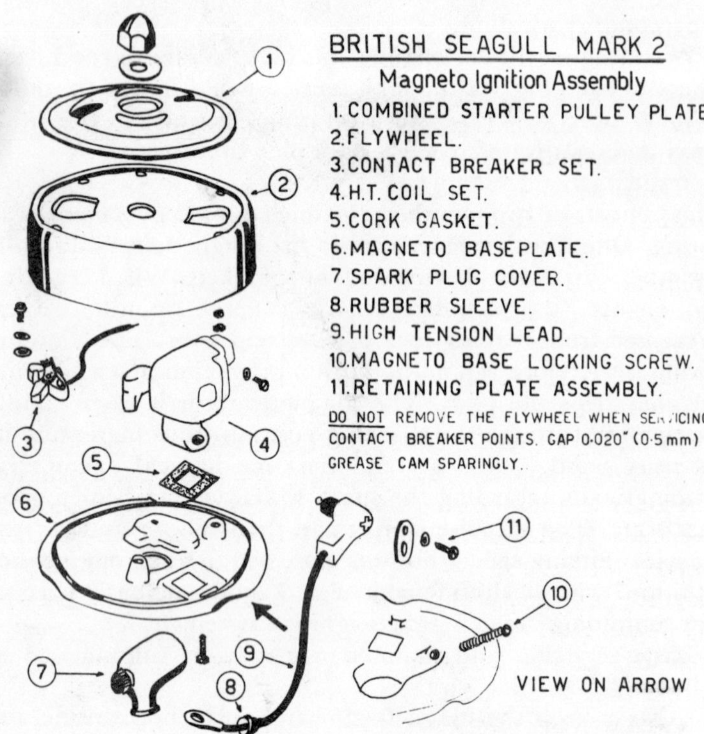

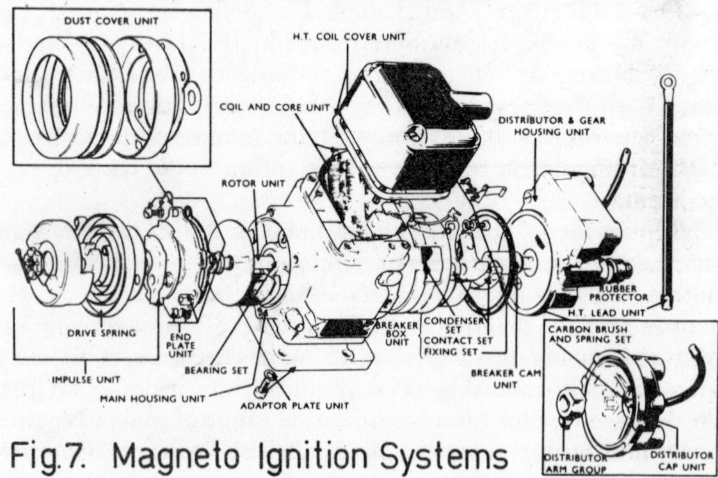

Fig.7. Magneto Ignition Systems

Victor and British Seagull. I am delighted to say this company will make every endeavour to renovate and repair obsolete magnetos they have manufactured in the past. Breaker gaps vary from 0.010in to 0.015in (Lucas-Wico) and 0.020in (British Seagull).

4. Lubrication is often necessary for some of the parts but great care is needed to see that the inside, especially the points and windings do NOT become fouled up with excess oil. Points to oil may include the contact breaker pivot post and cam grease pad (where fitted) using summer grade of motor transmission oil, bearings with high melting point grease, impulse starter springs with thin machine oil. With the smaller number of engine hours we run each season it is safe to say if we look after the lubrication once a year this will be sufficient.

5. High-tension cables harden with age and crack. This allows the spark to wander off anywhere but to the plug! Check the HT leads. Chafe may be caused by engine vibration, especially where they enter conduit. It is not unknown for the cable to look in perfect condition while in fact the conductor is broken. HT leads are sometimes held in place and contact made by securing screws which pierce the cable with a needle point. Do ensure the needle is sharp and not broken off and that it is screwed well home.

The Distributor (petrol engines inboard, outdrive and outboard)

Fig. 8 shows a simplified ignition circuit and distributor for a four-stroke four-cylinder petrol engine. Visual inspection at laying-up time can save an awful lot of trouble. Check that the high-tension leads from the head to the plugs are in good condition. They should be tight-fitting both into the plastic distributor head and onto the plugs. Sloppy fits may cause shorting while poor contacts reduce the spark to next to nothing. Old leads often crack and should be renewed with proper grade HT cable. If the plastic head has been damaged it must be replaced, as this would let dampness into the rotor area and cause shorting from the rotor to the body when the air is damp. The cap should for a similar reason be kept scrupulously clean. Inside the cap at the top you will find the

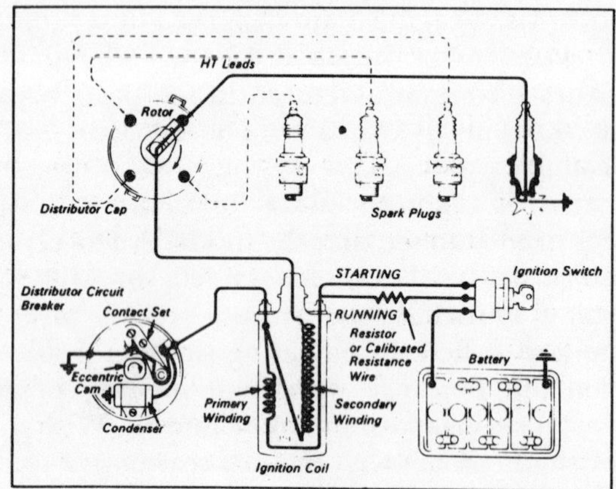

SIMPLIFIED IGNITION SYSTEM

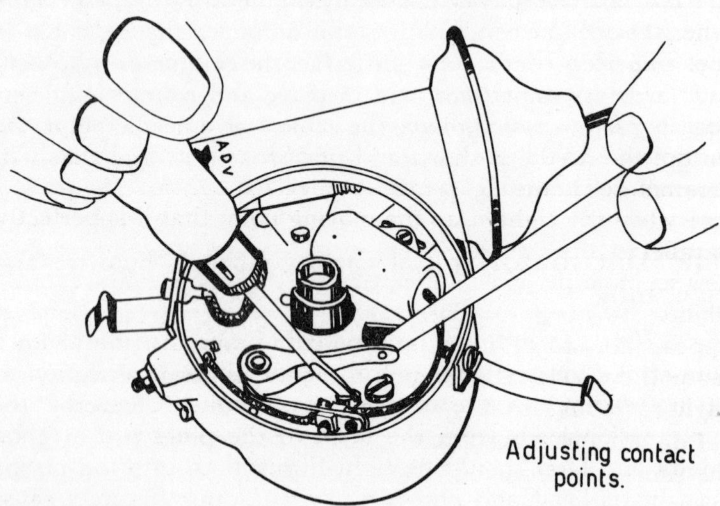

Adjusting contact points.

The Primary Circuit

When the distributor contact points close, current flows through the primary circuit from the battery via the ignition and solenoid switches, the ignition coil primary winding and the contact points and back to the battery via earth. (Note the resistor is by-passed during starting when maximum output is required.) Energy is stored in the coil in the form of a magnetic field.

Fig. 8. Ignition System Servicing

centrally sprung electrode that carries the high tension current down to the top of the rotor. This should not wobble and the spring must not have lost its tension. Some rotors have the contact spring on them (as in Fig. 8) and this bears onto a fixed central electrode. This spring, too, must be under proper tension or the rotor should be renewed. The rotor carries the current from the spring to each terminal in turn.

The rotor is easily removable and for this reason it is an excellent way of making a boat difficult to steal. Always have a spare rotor aboard. A little oil on the rotor shaft will eliminate the chance of rotor squeak. Below and on either side of the rotor you will find two more components of interest. First, a condenser which can, very rarely, fail but which is easily replaced if you carry a spare. A faulty condenser can cause contact point burning and reduce the secondary voltage output.

Secondly, you will find a pair of points which carry out a function like those I described in the magneto earlier. This time, though, there will be a number of high spots of cams that will open the contact points the same number of times each revolution as there are numbers of cylinders on the engine. The engine manual will tell you the correct gap to set the points with a feeler gauge. Only one contact will have to be loosened so that the gap can be correctly adjusted. Again, be sure when you tighten up the moving point that it is perfectly parallel to the other fixed contact. It is usual nowadays to fit a new set of points when any pitting occurs on the contact faces. Points in good condition should have a grey, frosted appearance. More confidence will be gained if the engine manual describes the fitting procedure in detail as there are slight variations from one make of petrol motor to another.

I do not advise the amateur to fiddle about with correcting the timing or servicing the timing of his petrol motor. The lower body of the distributor has a clamping nut that, when

---

The Secondary Circuit

When the contact points open, the primary circuit is broken and the condenser brings the current flow to an abrupt halt, absorbing current that would otherwise cause arcing at the points. The magnetic field collapses and a high voltage surge of up to 28,000 volts is produced in the secondary winding. This is delivered via the rotor and high tension lead to the spark plug, where a spark is produced across the electrodes, and the secondary circuit back to the battery is completed by the plug shell and earth.

undone, allows it to rotate about its own axis. All you should do is ensure this is always tight as any rotation will alter the timing, and unless you can get it back this will ruin the starting ability and performance of your engine.

There is one other part of the unit which you should know about: the automatic advance and retard system that looks after the job of getting the spark to the plug at the correct time when starting, but as the throttle is opened, getting it there just a shade earlier. Briefly, the suction at the carburettor causes a reduction in pressure in a small pipe running from the carburettor to a diaphragm. This diaphragm is linked mechanically to the plate which houses contact points. As the throttle is opened to speed up the engine, the contact points are rotated so that the cam lifts them a fraction of a second earlier. See that there is no mechanical damage to the tubing linking the diaphragm to the carburettor. If damage is suspected, removal of the tube at the carburettor and suction applied via your own mouth will soon check if you are able to move the contact plate a fraction of an inch. If there is no movement, suspect a fault in either the tubing or the diaphragm. If the diaphragm has failed, it means that the whole distributor will have to come off and the engine timing be disturbed, and is therefore a job for the fully equipped and skilled mechanic.

You can check the primary circuit of the ignition, which will be low voltage from the battery flowing via the ignition switch when it is turned on. A bulb in a holder connected with a couple of short wires is all you need. Attach one wire to the CB terminal of the coil and the other to earth on the engine body. If the primary circuit is working, the bulb will light when the contact points are open; as the points close it will go out. To check the secondary circuit, hold the HT lead which emerges from the top of the coil from the centre of the distributor head and as the engine is turned over a fat blue spark should jump a short distance from the end of the lead to the engine body. A word of warning: *never do this with petrol fumes around or you will blow yourself and the boat up.* Finally, see that the whole lot is replaced as you started, making sure the HT leads go back to the sparking plugs in the correct firing order.

Air Cleaners

A nice simple job for the amateur is to check that the air cleaner on the engine is in good condition. Both petrol and diesel engines use vast quantities of air and the cleaner makes sure it is safely cleaned to go into the engine. Perkins have found that their new type A.C. Air Filter also eliminates a good deal of intake noise, so the yachtsman with noise problems aboard might like to find out more about this aspect.

Engine air filters are of two types. The first is simply wire mesh in an inverted bowl. The whole filter can be washed in paraffin, allowed to drain down, then soaked and drained with engine oil. The oil on the wire catches the next lot of dirt. Then we have the paper element filters. These are very much more efficient and the paper element is replaced as a complete new unit. In my experience, unless you are operating in very dusty conditions, the element needs replacing only once every two years.

After winterisation all air intakes on an engine should be sealed up to keep out damp. Remember that the air intake is fitted as a 'flame trap' to prevent a backfire starting a serious fire outside the engine. Do not interfere with this function!

Cooling Systems

Two basic types of cooling are employed by petrol or diesel marine engines: they will be either air or water cooled. Water cooled units may be further subdivided, but these can be discussed under specific headings.

Air cooling

This depends for its efficiency on a plentiful volume of clean air being able to pass over the castings and special cooling fins on the cylinder head. You may find this type of cooling on a small outboard unit or on a huge marine diesel unit capable of driving a large fishing vessel or motor yacht. The great attraction of this type of cooling is its utter simplicity; no pipes, water passages, heat exchangers or pumps are needed. The cooling fins do, however, become clogged with debris and cleaning each fin on a cylinder head can be tedious work, but it is amazing how much dirt can be removed – even seagull feathers, as a friend of mine found out when his engine seriously overheated. No special treatment of this cooling system is needed at laying-up time – another advantage.

Direct water cooling systems

In this type of marine engine, the cooling water is taken directly into the cooling passageways of the engine castings from outside the boat. It is most often found in use on outboard engines and less elaborate inboard engines. The water may be that from a canal or sea-water. It is sometimes referred to as 'raw water' cooling. The water is drawn into the engine via a skin-fitting valve by a simple water pump usually of the Jabsco type. This is an impeller pump; it induces a suction as a rubber impeller is squeezed within a housing to eject the water into the engine; as it moves on past the cam, the resultant suction draws in more water. It is delightfully simple in action and well within the capabilities of the amateur mechanic to service (Fig. 9 shows the main working parts).

The end plate is easily removed and on it you will find the pump reference number. This is needed so that spare parts can be ordered. You will always need a supply of paper gaskets to go under the end plate so keep a good stock in hand. Next remove the impeller, which is usually made of neoprene rubber. It may be on a plain forked shaft or a splined one. Grip it with a pair of water-pump or round-nosed pliers near to the shaft and slide along till it is clear of the casting. Inspect the round section ends of the impeller for wear, and check that the blades themselves are not torn. A spare impeller should always be carried.

As the shaft is removed, inspect it for pitting corrosion, particularly where it lies under the seals. The shafts are often made of stainless steel and pitting attack occurs because of oxygen starvation. If attack has occurred, the neoprene seals will probably have been torn and will need replacing.

Next you should look to see if there is a 'slinger' washer. This slings away any water that has crept past the seal from the impeller housing. Again, if you find one, always carry a few slinger washers. All the spares except the shaft and impeller cost very little, so a stock is not going to break you.

You may find different versions of the Jabsco type pump I

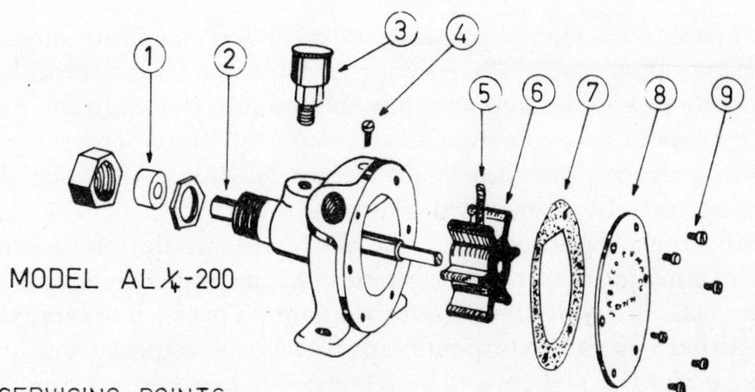

SERVICING POINTS

1. Gland packing - renew if leaks occur along shaft. Do not over tighten gland nut. Pumps using metal cup/rubber shaft need service replacemet of seal when worn or damaged.
2. S/S shafts may suffer corrosionattack under seals.
3. Do not forget to give the greaser a turn when one is fitted.
4. Cam screw. Keep tight - use jointing compound on the thread.
5. Impeller screw gives drive from forked shafts. Other shafts are splined to provide drive.
6. Impeller - always carry spares
7. Paper gasket - keep spares.
8. End cover - note model number for ordering spares. Service kits are available.
9. End cover screws - loosen for simple drain down.

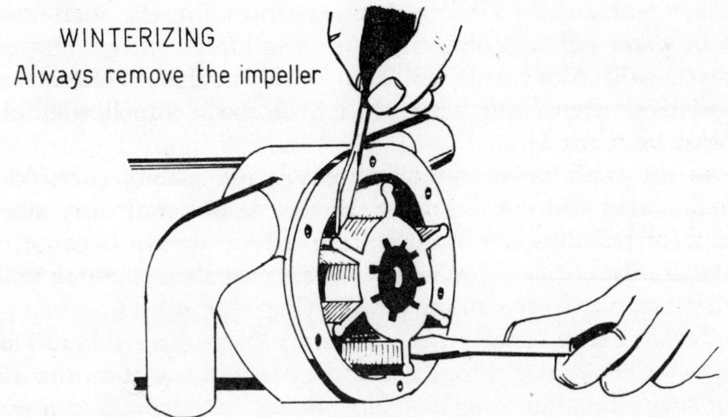

Fig. 9 Jabsco pump servicing.

have described, but engine manuals will describe these and the basic points I have made will apply. On some units the rubber seals are in a metal cup which is pressed into the main casting. They can be prised out with a couple of small screwdrivers working from either side, but be careful not to damage the casting with the screwdriver blades.

This type of pump is used for raw water circulation on both direct and indirect cooled engines, as the impeller is able to cope with gritty debris without damage. This is, however, the stuff that causes the impeller tips to wear, so expect trouble if your boat takes the ground regularly!

Winterising the Jabsco pump. Remove end plate and impeller. This will prevent permanent deformation of the compressed section of the impeller blades. Dry out all water and, provided service has been satisfactory, grease the shaft. Don't be too liberal with grease on the shaft as normal mineral oil will soon ruin neoprene impellers. The safest grease is Marfak 2HD which can be used on both shaft and housing; this ensures that the impeller will not get damaged by running dry on putting the engine into service again. I use ordinary grease on the shaft and glycerine pinched from the medicine cabinet on the housing. Glycerine is quite safe to lubricate the impeller.

Raw water cooling winterisation. The main enemy is corrosion when the water is drained down for the winter. If fresh water can be connected onto the intake valve while the craft is still afloat, this will help flush out debris and is very beneficial where salt water has been the cooling medium. Damp salt on metal will give rise to fearful corrosion problems, and I have seen wet liner engines have their cylinder walls eaten through in just a few seasons of use when winterisation has been inadequate. Make up a rust-proofing mixture using five parts water to one part Esso Cutwell 40 or Shell Donax C, or similar emulsifying type oil. (You need a larger quantity for a larger engine.) Disconnect the suction pipe at the intake valve on the engine and insert it into the bucket after the engine has been run up to normal temperature. Then run the engine again so that the water/oil emulsion is drawn into the engine to coat the internal water passages. Stop the engine immediately the solution is drawn from the bucket as running the pump dry will damage it. The warm engine will now dry the rust-proofing solution onto the internal parts and so protect them. Do read the maker's handbook and use your eyes to see that every drain tap has been opened and check that any water plugs on gearboxes or reduction gears have been drained down as well. All orifices must be thoroughly dry and a de-watering aerosol should be used to keep taps free and ensure threads on plug holes do not corrode. Many engines have cathodic protection against corrosion. Check this and renew any cathode elements you find if they are more than half eaten away.

Indirect cooling systems

These work on the principle that fresh water collects the heat from the engine and transfers it to raw water via either a heat exchanger or keel cooling pipes. The advantage of this type of cooling is that highly corrosive warm salt water is not in contact with the main body of the engine. The fresh water is self-contained in a closed circuit consisting of the header tank, heat exchanger, water passages and circulating pump. A second pump of the impeller type circulates the raw water through a heat exchanger and sometimes through a second heat exchanger which cools the gearbox oil and is then discharged overboard. The raw water is usually used to cool exhaust gases at an injection bend on its passage overboard. Technically speaking this system, though more expensive than raw water cooling, has much to recommend it. The engine can be designed to run at a specific temperature, corrosion problems are reduced, local overheating due to scaling in narrow passageways is eliminated and oils will not be so prone to sludging, so reducing engine wear. The price you have to pay is in higher initial cost and a slightly more complex system to maintain. Let us look at each part of the indirect system and see where it must be given attention.

The raw water section. Basically, this is the same as that described in raw water cooled engines and needs to be given the same maintenance and winterisation as that already described. A real bother spot to watch out for in both types of cooling system is where the raw water is injected into the exhaust stream at the water injection bend: beware of impingement corrosive attack. The metal in the bend corrodes with the hot sea water rapidly but this is made even worse when the high velocity water knocks off the corrosion and leaves new metal exposed to similar attack. You can be certain that one spare really worth having aboard is a spare injection bend!

The header tank. Room has to be provided for water expansion and, to allow the fresh water to reach a higher than normal boiling temperature, it is put under pressure. The filling orifice is closed by a pressure cap and a small overflow pipe is provided so that if the system is overfilled the excess water escapes safely via the cap down a drain pipe fitted to the side of the filler neck. Check that the rubber pipe is not perished and that it leads excess water out of the way of the engine or rust will soon be a problem just below it! The pressure cap itself must seat cleanly so that it can build up pressure in the system, but there is another valve in the cap which prevents a vacuum building up in the system by allowing air to return into the header tank as the engine cools down. The cap is often handled and sometimes, because its important functions are not realised, it is abused.

If you have overheating, pinking on petrol motors, boiling or excessive coolant loss, first check the pressure cap. Run the engine up to working temperature and stop it. Taking great care about the possibility of boiling water scalding you, place a large cloth over the pressure cap and another over your hand and gently turn back the cap. You should hear the release of pressure clearly if the cap is sealing the system properly. Remove cap fully only when pressure is down and examine it for worn or damaged parts. Look at the condition of the sealing gasket and the locking diaphragm. Check that the secondary gasket on some pressure caps is intact and replace if worn.

Thermostats. These are found on both types of water cooling system and their function is to regulate the flow of water round the cylinder block so that the engine reaches its correct working temperature as quickly as possible and then maintains it. When the engine is cold, the thermostat restricts the flow of coolant until it reaches a pre-determined temperature. Don't worry about the water injection into the exhaust suffering, as a by-pass is arranged so that water will continuously be available for that purpose. When the correct temperature is reached, a small quantity of wax contained in a copper cup rapidly expands and exerts pressure through a synthetic rubber surround onto a specially shaped piston which is fixed at its top end to a rigid frame. The wax pellet is thus forced downward, opening the thermostat valve which is attached to it, against a spring pressure, allowing the coolant to flow freely. Thermostats must always be checked if abnormally high or low temperatures are registering on temperature gauges and all else appears to be well. The wax pellet may have failed, trapped dirt may prevent the valve from seating properly, or the valve may have become gummed up with sludge in the cooling system.

Location of the thermostat on the engine will vary but, unless stated otherwise in the handbook, look at the forward end of the main cylinder block casting (Fig. 10). It may be hidden in the block under the header tank or it may be easily accessible right on top, as in some Volvo engines. You will have to drain off all coolant and after gaining access to the unit, lift it out carefully, prising with a screwdriver under its flange, *not* under the valve. If it looks worn or distorted throw it away but if, after careful cleaning, things look all right, dunk it in hot water with a temperature about 11°C less than the temperature marked on the flange. As the water temperature is increased the valve should begin to open progressively until there is at least ¼in (0.6cm) of movement at a temperature of about 11°C in excess of that marked. Clean the seating where the thermostat is to be replaced and re-assemble either with the one that has passed this simple test or with a new one.

Rubber hoses are all too often a part of marine engine cooling systems and really are a weakness that must always be countered. They perish and harden with age and could let one down disastrously. Rubber hoses may be specially moulded to form bends, or made of straight section rubber. Always keep a couple of feet of straight rubber hose of the correct ply so that short lengths can be cut off for replacements. There is no way out of having a good spares supply of shaped rubber connectors. Only ever use stainless steel hose clips and keep some spares handy.

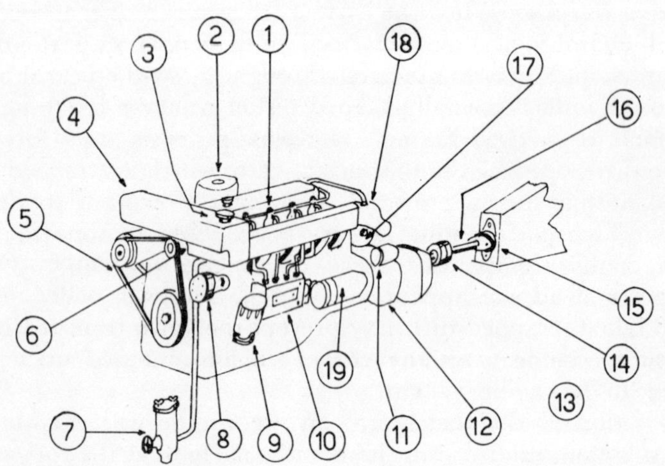

1. Injectors.
2. Air cleaner filter.
3. Cooling water filler cap.
4. Cooling system flushing.
5. Generator and drive belt.
6. Thermostat.
7. Raw water valve and strainer.
8. Jabsco pump.
9. Engine oil filter.
10. Fuel injection pump, filters.
11. Gear box oil filter.
12. Gear box oil.
13. Reduction box oil.
14. Flexible couplings.
15. Inboard gland packing.
16. Shaft for corrosion and wear.
17. Heat exchanger.
18. Exhaust cooling injection bend.
19. Starter.

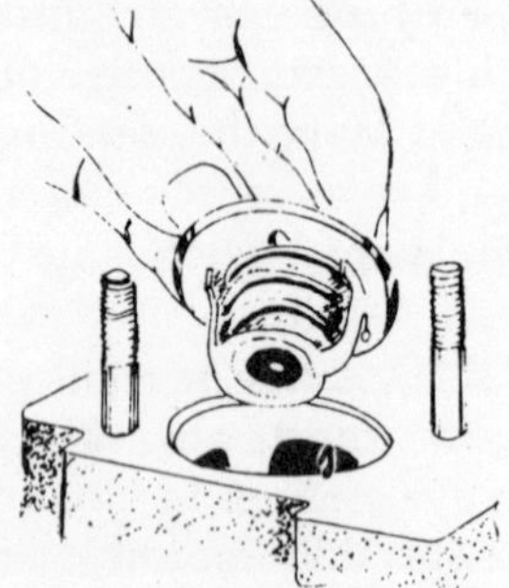

Thermostat found here in the cylinder block.

Heat exchanger for water or oil cooling.

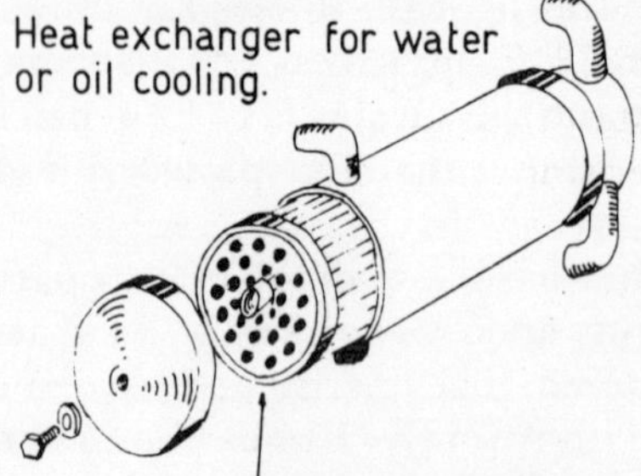

Clean tube stack.

Fig.10. Diesel installation parts commonly found needing maintenance.

The heat exchanger (Fig. 10). This has two lots of water passing through it – that from the closed fresh water circuit and the raw water that is to remove the heat from it. Locate the unit on the engine and service it annually at lay-up time when the cooling system is drained down. The unit consists of a casting (sometimes the actual header tank) with a stack of tubes passing through it. End caps unbolt to reveal sealing rings, which stop the unit from leaking and keep the raw water apart from the fresh. The fresh water section will usually look quite clean, but the raw water, especially if salty and contaminated, will have gunged up the tube stack. Light soiling can be dealt with by passing a knitting needle down the tubes in the opposite direction to the normal flow while the unit is immersed in clean water. Do not prod dirt too hard or you will damage the tubes.

On badly maintained engines, the whole of the fresh water circuit may be fouled up. If this is so, drain the system down and, while afloat, fill the system with a proprietary cleaning agent in solution with water to top up the system to its normal level. If you can't get a proprietary product you can make up a 3 per cent solution of citric or tartaric acid. It may be necessary to run the engine for several hours to clear heavy scaling and to empty the system and re-top it with clear solution until a satisfactory state of cleanliness is reached. Drain off the solution and replace it with a 1 per cent solution of sodium carbonate (washing soda) or sodium tetraborate (borax) to neutralise the acid. Run the engine for five to ten minutes then drain off. You can now safely refill with a winterising anti-freeze solution or leave it drained down.

Anti-freeze in marine engines should conform to the manufacturers' recommendations and, preferably, conform to BS3151. This is quite safe for the closed circuit pump that circulates it. The pump itself is usually of the centrifugal type and is not in the repair province of the amateur mechanic since special tools are invariably needed to take it apart.

Engine Oils

Modern marine engines for pleasure boating generally get their power from high revolutions. This does enable them to be kept extremely compact but puts extra burdens on the oils which lubricate them. Higher stresses and increased working temperatures have meant that oil specifications have to be made to maintain viscosities from cold to hot conditions and thus have 'viscosity index improvers' added; the multigrade oils manage this. They also have to have 'anti-oxident' additives which ensure that as the oil sprays onto journals, washes round the engine and is brought into intimate mixture with air it does not oxidise and lose its lubricating properties. The products of combustion-acids, carbon, gases and water vapour leak past the bottom rings of pistons and are deposited on the internal parts of the engine, crankcase walls, oil passageways and the sump, where it would sludge up the works if it were not for detergent additives which wash off the sludge and stop any seizure that would occur if the working parts were starved of oil.

Another additive, a dispersant, keeps all the sludge particles in suspension till the filter removes the larger, dangerous ones so that they don't scour the bearings and working surfaces of the engine. One more additive is probably present in a premium oil and that is an anti-wear one. This is to protect small components under great stress from premature wear; cams, tappets and valve guides are thus taken care of.

All these additives get used up in the course of the season. An anti-oxident can only deal with a given amount of oxygen and an anti-wear additive with so much severe stress. This is why you should renew the oil in the engine after as little as a hundred engine hours, or at the end of the season, and according to manufacturers' instructions thereafter. We put extra demands on oil because we run engines so little and for comparatively short periods; also there is salt in the atmosphere and sometimes wind-blown sand (silica). With a marine engine costing so much these days, a gallon or so of fresh oil is a very small insurance premium to pay for a long serviceable life.

With all these additives already present in a premium oil, there is no point in adding a whole lot of oily potions that are supposed to work miracles. However, I believe products which have molybdenum disulphide can be extremely useful when rebuilding an engine and especially when rebuilding racing engines. On initial starting, these molybdenum particles give instant lubrication to surfaces that would in that instant be oil starved. They should *never* be used on new engines as it is wise to let working surfaces gradually bed down and hone themselves to a perfect mirror finish during running in. Yes, it seems terrible to realise that small metal particles ground off the pistons, cylinder walls and bearings are scouring round the engine, but there is no need to worry as the main filter will deal with them safely. It is, then, vital after a short running-in period to renew both oil and filter so that the now polished surfaces can receive the royal treatment from brand new oil with all its additives present and not a sign of metal particles. Never leave filthy oil in the engine over winter!

Gear oils

Different types of marine gearbox will need different types of oil. Some may use exactly the same as that recommended for the engine while others will need oils specifically developed for the gear-box or reduction gear. It is thus vital to look at the gear-box and reduction gear oil specification. Special gear oils often contain a foam suppressant as the whirling gear really can work some oils into a lather. They are often designed to cope with extreme pressures and 'E.P.' additives are called for in some bevel gear systems. Hypoid gears often found on outboard engines at the bottom end often require hypoid oils, as this type of gear induces really heavy loadings initiating extreme pressures.

Greases

The marine mechanic's armoury is not complete without knowing about and having to hand specialist greases for use aboard the yacht, not only for the engine but for general lubricating jobs such as shackle pins, rigging screws, etc. Modern greases consist of metallic soap mixed with a lubricating oil. Lithium soap is the basis of most multipurpose greases. Specialist greases have been developed for specific functions which the yachtsman must know about. If you trail your boat, High Melting Point grease may be called for in the trailer wheel bearings. Water pumps may require a waterproof grease, while underwater we may need a highly adhesive waterproof grease. It is thus essential to read the engine manual for specifications for the correct grease to use in maintenance. Never use grease where oil is specified.

Specialist oils

We create problems for boats because we lay them up for the winter. When mechanical units - engines, pumps, valves, generators - stand idle for a long period in the most trying weather, they need careful protection from the ravages of corrosion, chemical attack (remember those acids in the exhaust) and the weathering so many boats undergo in the open. I shall be dealing explicitly with winterising in later chapters but, again, the oil companies have developed a whole range of oil products which are really excellent for prolonging the life of yacht machinery.

'Storage' or 'preservative' oils are put into the sump to protect internal working surfaces from corrosion. They often give off vapour to inhibit the atmosphere in cylinders, manifolds and crankcases. Diesel fuel systems demand protection from diesel fuel system corrosion inhibiting oils. Under certain conditions, diesel fuel 'waxes' up and can block the fine parts to be found in the injection system. These are, in any case, made to such wonderfully fine limits that the slightest bit of corrosion from water particles in fuel will damage them beyond repair. Your favourite oil company will be only too pleased to give you a full list of specialist oils that really are worth attention; they usually give you a booklet with complete information, so why not write off for one?

Flushing oils are designed to clean out the engine before lay-up oils are added. Some engineers assert that if you use them they are likely to show up weaknesses in oil seals and let them leak. Quite honestly, if the engine and gear-box oil seals are staying leak free only because they are sludged up then it is high time they were renewed. Companies making these oils give precise instructions as to their specific application and use, and this should be followed carefully.

Aerosol lubricants and preservatives

A word of caution regarding the use of 'secret formula' aerosols that have become available in recent years and which claim to be the miracle answer to corrosion and lubrication problems. Although many of them may live up to their claims in protecting metal, when used in marine applications where different types of materials are in close proximity, they can produce unfortunate compatibility problems. For example, some may contain silicones. These are excellent from the point of view of moisture displacement and lubrication properties, but are the very devil to remove if you have oversprayed onto GRP, which might need to have new bonding or repairs done to it.

Another worry is the fact that in order to thin some very worthwhile lubricants to a spraying consistency, some manufacturers use chlorinated solvents. Despite what is said, these can interfere with rubbers and plastics, sometimes causing brittleness or hardening. US Government research recommends that hydrocarbon-based solvent should be used where plastics are concerned. At this moment I am prepared to recommend the following commercial products for marine applications which, if used as instructed, will give entirely satisfactory results:

Rocket WD-40	Chlorinated solvent	Only on metal surfaces for dewatering and corrosion inhibiting
CRC	Chlorinated solvent	As above
Duckham's Dry Spark	Trichlorethelyne	Trichlorethelyne must only be used in very well ventilated spaces and not in contact with the skin. Silicone-based, so don't overspray. Excellent waterproofing
LPS	Hydrocarbon solvent	Universal application

You would be well advised to get the manufacturers' literature to check application data, and do ensure that there is good ventilation when using aerosol cans as their contents can in adverse circumstances be a health hazard.

Lubrication System Servicing

A messy job but well within the capabilities of the average yachtsman. You need shallow tins to contain the oil draining from the minute spaces found beneath the gearbox and reduction gears. It is useful when manufacturers put on a sump-emptying hand pump, but I have blessed the gearbox-makers who make life awkward with inaccessible sump plugs! The following procedures should be used in conjunction with the engine manual.

1. When changing oil always run the engine up to working temperature so that sludge and debris are well stirred up ready to be pumped out.
2. Wipe all dirt from around filters that are to be replaced so that it does not get into the system.
3. Flushing oil poured up to the lower level of the dipstick is all that is required to get the real grime out of the system. Run the engine for ten minutes or so with *no load at a fastish idle.* Their lubrication properties are not designed for fast or heavy load conditions.
4. Pump out all flushing oil from main sump. Gearboxes and reduction gears do not need flushing but at this stage they should have their oil removed too.
5. Remove old filters and have an old biscuit tin or plastic bag handy to drop them into. Filters will be one of two types: the replaceable element or the 'spin on' complete unit. The latter is favoured on modern engines but is a bit more expensive. A new filter of either type comes complete with gaskets.
6. Clean off the seating where the filter is to go.
7. With element filters, fit the square section rubber gasket very carefully, ensuring it is not twisted, then fit the filter in its body. With spin-on filters, lightly grease the gasket on the filter and the seating, and only do them up hand-tight so that future removal will be easier. 'Wipac' make an excellent tool for removing obstinate spin on filters. Do any gearbox oil filter at the same time as the main engine filter.
8. Bring all oil levels in engine, gearbox and reduction gear (if fitted) to their normal recommended levels.
9. Run the engine for a few minutes and leave for at least another ten after stopping to allow oils to drain down.

10. Check oil levels, which will have gone down because the filters are now full of the new oil. Bring up to proper level on the dipstick. Run the engine up to working temperature and check for leaks.

Winterisation of lubrication systems

The previous procedure is followed except that a preservative engine oil is added instead of the normal grade. This is drained down at the beginning of the season and normal oil used for replenishment. On some engines you will find an oil cooler. This works in principle like the heat exchanger we discussed earlier.

Diesel Engine Maintenance and Winterisation

Fig. 10 shows the parts that are likely to need your attention. The information given so far concerning cooling, lubrication, air cleaners, oils, etc. is equally applicable to the marine diesel engine. However, instead of spark ignition and the electrical system, there is a complex fuel system which pressurises diesel fuel to an enormous pressure and at a precise moment delivers a minute quantity of it into the cylinder via injectors. Under compression, this fuel burns to give the power stroke. The fuel equipment is made to extremely fine tolerances and is quite beyond the amateur to service, but we can carry out some work which will help maintain the system in first-class condition.

1. All parts of the fuel system should be kept scrupulously clean. On all installations, the fuel tanks and pipework should be cleaned out at the end of each season.
2. Fuel filters (the best systems have two) should be maintained with new elements each season. See Fig. 11 for typical layout of filters.
3. Winterisation of the fuel system is highly recommended. It entails introducing special preservative oils (ESSO IL815, ESSO IL1047, Shell Calibration Fluid 'C' (in UK), Shell Calibration Fluid 'B' (overseas) or Shell Fusus 'A' into the system. This is most easily done if a pre-filter is fitted by either disconnecting the fuel intake pipe and making up a reservoir attachment, or by screwing an attachment into one of the alternative inlets usually found on these filters. Fill the

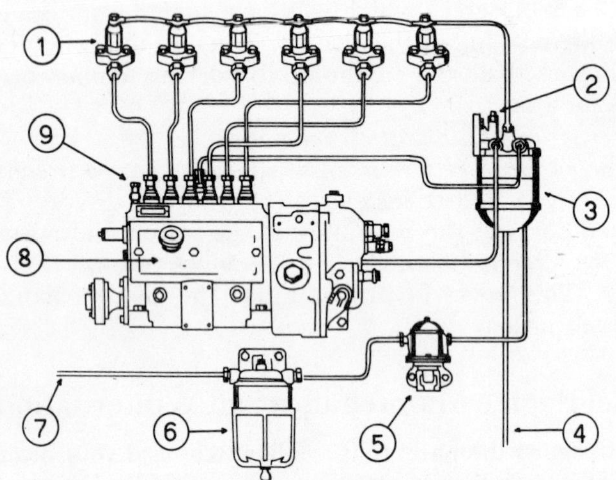

Diesel engine fuel system using INLINE injection pump.

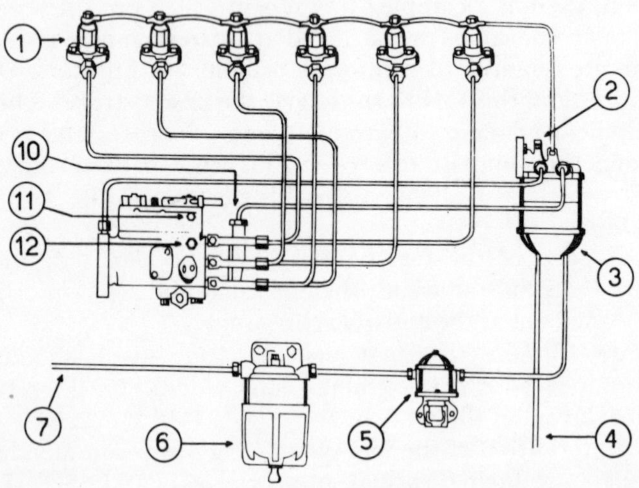

Diesel engine fuel system using C.A.V. mechanically governed DPA pump. Note that hydraulically governed pumps have the governor vent located on the end.

Fig.11. Diesel Fuel Systems

Fig. 11. Diesel Fuel Systems

1. Injectors need professional servicing but can be tested by the owner.
2. Engine service filter (usualy built on) requires new element and bleeding via screw on the top. Bleed by undoing screw and working AC fuel pump by hand till fuel flows clear of air bubbles. Then tighten down.
3. Service filter elements should be carried as spares.
4. Excess fuel feed back to fuel tank.
5. AC-Delco Fuel Pump. Clean filter in top.
6. Preliminary filter separates water and sediment from fuel. Regularly drain off water and change filter element each season. Strongly recommended to fit one if not already built into the fuel system.
7. Line to fuel tank. The whole fuel system should be winterised with special fuel additives and the tank sealed (including breather) to minimise condensation and rain water getting into fuel tank.
8. INLINE pump elements can be reached under this cover and worked up and down to bleed air from high pressure lines and injectors.
9. Vent plug for fuel gallery.
10. DPA pump fuel inlet union vent.
11. Vent on governor housing of DPA mechanically governed pump.
12. Vent valve on hydraulic head.

---

reservoir with the preservative oil and run the engine until the system is full. The engine will run on these oils so there is no need to worry about cleaning them out. On small installations, the easiest method to introduce them is to drain down the fuel tank, clean it out, then put the oil into that and run the engine in the normal way.

Bleeding fuel systems

If any air is introduced into the fuel system on a diesel engine it will not start or run. Every engine manual gives specific instructions for doing this job, and Lucas Marine or C.A.V. Ltd. (Lucas/CAV Group) will supply an excellent booklet *CAV marine diesel fuel injection equipment for the boat owner* and, incidentally, one on marine electrical systems, both of which give really valuable information.
which give really valuable information.

Fig. 11 shows diagramatic sketches of the two basic types of diesel fuel system. The main principle to follow is to bleed from the fuel tank towards the injectors. If you have a bad memory, paint the bleed screws with a dab of coloured paint so that you can quickly identify them. The low pressure side of the system can be fed and bled by actuating the fuel pump (often A.C.-Delco type) until the injection pump is full and air free. The high pressure side from injection pump to injectors is bled by loosening a couple of high pressure pipes at the injector and working the injection pump manually in the case of 'inline' type or by means of the starter motor turning the whole engine over with the DPA type. The pump elements of the 'inline' pump can be worked up and down by means of a screwdriver from the pump gallery, taking care not to damage any internal parts.

Injectors and Pipework

Servicing injectors is a job for the specialist. For the average yacht, well maintained, a three year service period will usually be sufficient unless trouble is being experienced. To check injectors, they should be carefully removed from the engine by disconnecting their high pressure supply, the two nuts holding them in place and the bleed back pipe. Never strain any of the pipes or unions as they are dismantled, for getting them back will then be a difficult job and may result in damage. Reverse the injectors on the high pressure pipes so they will spray away from the engine. Do *not* get your hands in front of the spray from the nozzles or they might inject you with diesel fuel! Look for an even spray pattern with no dribbling as the engine is turned over on the starter. Any doubts about the pattern of spray, dribbling or no sharp cut off of the spray should be dealt with by servicing at an approved station. Re-inserting the injectors needs care for they must go down onto their seats perfectly. Some injectors have gaskets under them like spark plugs and others go directly onto the engine casting. If gaskets are used, get new ones and carry spares for such occasions. Replace pipework and bleed the system.

A leak in pipework on any type of engine must never be tolerated. Petrol is explosive and diesels do not like air, so a regular check on all pipework should be carried out.

Exhaust Systems

I deliberately left exhaust systems till last so that these would stay fresh in your mind, for if there is one place to look for trouble it is here. I have already mentioned the main trouble spot in the raw water section of the cooling system – the injection bend. Other systems employ a 'dry' exhaust which has to be lagged until it is clear of the boat and then it discharges straight into the atmosphere. Both are subject to the most intense corrosion you will ever encounter for the following reasons.

1. All carbon fuels produce water vapour when burnt and even in a dry exhaust it is in fact wet enough to keep the walls of the piping saturated after the engine is stopped.

2. Elevated temperatures greatly accelerate corrosive chemical reactions between the combustion vapours and the metal.

3. The high velocity of cooling water impinging onto the metal walls of the exhaust injection bend and pipework removes products of corrosion at such a rate that new metal is constantly presented for accelerated attack. Combustion gases are usually acidic and form such delightful products as sulphuric acid. The exhaust system thus becomes the weakest part of any yacht engine installation.

4. There is always build-up of carbon and combustion products in any type of engine where gases pass through sharp bends. Carbon build-up results in back-pressure, which makes fuel consumption higher and/or loses power. To overcome these problems you need regular attention which must be given at lay-up time when the engine is winterised. Adopt the following procedures.

a) Drain every drop of water from the pipework. 'Dry' exhausts must have a drain tap at their lowest point. 'Wet' exhaust pipes should be disconnected at the manifold and their lowest point drained.

b) Decarbonisation should be done every second season from the manifold through to the injection bend. The injection bend must be attended to annually. After removing pipework or flanged joints see that they are treated with a preservative on flange faces, studs and couplings. There is nothing worse than fighting nuts and couplings which are thoroughly rusted up and you always end up smashing both yourself and engine with a large bill for penetrating oil. This oil is good but should never be needed on a properly maintained system.

Gaskets

You should always have plenty of gaskets to hand. Leaking exhaust gas will kill you or the occupants of a cabin if it gets in there. New gaskets are needed each season when the exhaust system's parts are rebuilt together. Gaskets can be made in an emergency by laying a sheet of the correct gasket material over the metal part needing the gasket and tapping all over the outline and parts to be cut out with an engineer's ball pein hammer. Once the outline is there a cutting knife will finish the job.

Preservation treatments

These will only slow down corrosive attack and then only with limited applications where temperatures suit products available. I have experimented with epoxy resin lining to wet bends to reduce impingement attack but this is only applicable where the exhaust is cool, as at the skin fitting end on wet systems. Perkins introduced an aluminium alloy water injection casting with annular injection rather than a single pipe impinging directly onto the casting wall. This is much more successful and a treatment with 'Little Ship' etch primer, followed by two-can polyurethane, has lasted two seasons with no corrosive damage to the casting at all. The same paint system has lasted two seasons on the outside of the hot section from manifold to injection bend with slight discolouration and only very superficial rust on iron castings. With renewal of the paint, the system should last several years, which I would guarantee could not happen with untreated units.

Engine Names and Numbers

Your engine may go under another name in a country you are visiting. Instead of being held up for weeks on a cruise waiting for spares, you can get to know about this from the manufacturer. Also, items like filters often have exact equivalents from different manufacturers. List these in your log book and you will be delighted how easy it is to get spares! So long as they are well-known manufacturers you need have no fear, although makers do like you to use their approved brand.

Chapter 7

THE ELECTRICAL SYSTEM AND ELECTRONIC GEAR

Both diesel and petrol marine engines have certain components in common.

Starter Motors

Unless submerged in water, dripped on or abused by cranking with reduced voltage and an over-heavy thumb, they are extremely reliable and will only need professional servicing at intervals of about five years for the average user who puts in two hundred engine hours each season.

Always listen out for good engagement of the starter motor gear with the flywheel and a smart turn over every time you press the button. Check that the cables from battery to starter are dry (not in bilge water) and tight, with no signs of chafe. Weak springs on sliding components within the motor may cause poor working-engagement and disengagement which could lead to serious damage. Spray with a suitable preservative aerosol to keep them in good condition with no verdigris on terminals. A solenoid unit (an electro-magnetic switch) is used to activate the starter motor and, again, this should have visual inspection to see that contacts are good and preserved. Check that the aerosol preservative really is safe on electrical wiring as mineral oils and some chemicals can damage it.

Winterisation can simply be sealing off open parts with

masking tape to keep oil vapour in and damp out. Always disconnect electrical power at the battery before removal for servicing. Removal of a cover plate allows access to check brush wear, which must conform to manufacturer's recommendations.

Alternators and Dynamos

Again, very reliable units and so long as they are registering a proper charge when the engine is running they need little attention. If things are not right you will need professional servicing.

Dynamos

These need inspection of wiring and brushes. Reference must again be made to manufacturers' recommendations. Brushes may be cleaned in carbon tetrachloride if they seem to be sticking. Ensure springs are not weak, thus ensuring good even contact with the commutator. Put the brush back in its holder in exactly the same way after removal (see Fig. 12 for details).

Some components require lubrication while others have sealed lubrication that requires no attention at all except major overhauls every two years. If oiling is called for, do this sparingly. On all types of unit make sure you replace covers precisely to keep dirt and water out.

Alternators

These are sensitive and easily damaged. They must never be 'flashed' or run without being fully connected into the electrical system, have a 'fast charger' connected via a dockside unit to help get a start, have polarity (+ and −) reversed, be 'Megger' tested or have a lead disconnected from the system while the engine is running. In case all that frightens you, they have been adopted into the marine world because they are basically simpler devices than the dynamo and give superior performance with less moving parts; thus they are more reliable than dynamos. They usually come with a 'fast fuse' unit which will blow if reverse polarity is applied accidentally. Know where the fast fuse is and carry spares. If a fuse blows, check polarity of connections before blowing another as they are quite expensive.

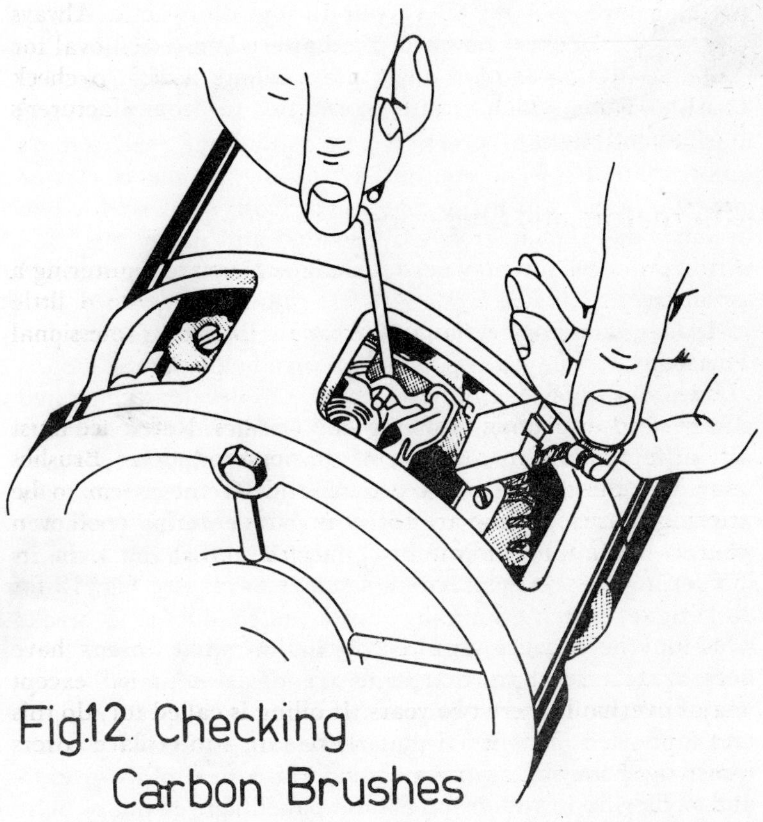

Fig.12. Checking Carbon Brushes

Drive belts

These will be found in use with alternators, dynamos and, occasionally, pumps. They do not take kindly to oil and should be kept clean. Their tension is very important. If they are over-tight they will damage the bearings of the machines. As a rough guide, about ½in (1.3cm) deflection on the longest run will be adequate. If you can press the belt in more than this with your thumb, the belt is probably too slack then slipping and wear will be increased. This is one 'spares' item that must always be carried. They are easily replaced by slacking off the retaining nuts on the unit they are driving, cleaning the pulleys and replacing the belt. Adjust the tension following the maker's recommendations or as I have suggested.

Wiring

Undoubtedly the major culprit where trouble is concerned. The blame must be laid squarely on two sources. First, bad marine installation practices; secondly, the yachtsman's unfortunate habit of continually adding to the electronic gadgetry he has aboard so that a marginally successful system becomes one that is grossly overloaded and dangerous. Bad wiring practices you may need to deal with can be summarised as follows.

1. Inadequate cross section to the conductor wires for the job. This leads to voltage drop, which in turn helps electric motors to burn out quicker and never be able to develop their rated power. Starter motors, water pumps, electric deck winches will suffer if the cross section of the wire being used is not related to the distance it has to conduct the electricity. Get your marine electrician to measure voltage at the terminals where a new appliance is to be connected so that you are sure it is getting the voltage it is designed for.

2. Fatigue, which eventually causes the conductor to break. This may be because terminals of the crimped variety have been squashed so hard that some strands are actually broken when they are made or because wiring is improperly clipped and supported. This is particularly bad on some GRP yachts, where the poor old electrician has nothing to clip his wires to and so they hang and droop behind panelling well out of sight of the unsuspecting yachtsman. A worthwhile maintenance job is to take panelling down and spend some time fixing up such loose wiring with plastic tape for the initial hold, then a bridge of glass tape resined over it.

3. Ventilation. All wiring likes to be kept cool and I will have much more to say on ventilation in Chapter 8, but in the meantime realise that alternator output drops with temperature rise. The engineers who design alternators take this into account, but *all* electrical equipment will be happier if there is dry air movement around it. Damp wiring can leak current and salt water can travel up a conductor and seriously corrode it. Havoc in the form of electrolytic corrosion will follow a leak to earth down a propeller shaft! Anything to do with electrics on a boat should be out of the way of weather

and drips. Wire connectors must always be completely weather-proofed by binding with insulating tape and then sealing completely with a quick setting silicone rubber compound, usually sold in small tubes.

Although you may have little confidence in yourself as a marine electrician, you can check and even renew wiring if you have carefully labelled each wire before it is renewed. I use either a 'Dymo' label printing machine or a small piece of postcard sealed under a strip of Sellotape. I'm no electrician so I draw diagrams, with wire colours, of any instrument I remove a wire from *before* I remove the wire.

Wiring harness

This has been a blessing in simplifying the wiring of marine engines as it has foolproof connectors at both engine and instrument panel ends. It still needs protection from chafe, proper support and clean connector terminals, so this should receive your attention at least at the beginning and end of the season.

Instrument Panels

These vary from one installation to another, but they really are meant to be looked at all the time and immediately there is a deviation from the normal by one of the instruments, it must be investigated and the real reason why it has deviated found and corrected. The instruments may be of the 'clock' type with a pointer, or simply a bulb that lights up to give warning. Bulbs are a bit of a menace as the filament can fail - carry spare bulbs. The nose, a human instrument much out of fashion these days, can really work wonders in discovering engine malfunctions if it is trained and used regularly!

Ignition (petrol) or generator warning lights come on when the key is inserted in a key-operated switch and glows red until the generator cuts in and extinguishes it. If it comes on other than when first starting, suspect a broken circuit, a blown fuse or a broken generator drive belt. It is not unknown for a switch to fail, so do a drawing of the wiring, remove it to an electrician's and if it fails a test, replace with a new one.

Ammeters indicate whether there is charging or discharging in the electrical system. With light switches on it should show a negative discharge, and when you start up, a positive one. If the instrument shows no current flow but the needle remains stationary at zero while all the wiring is working, you probably need a new one. Do not get wires reversed or you will show a charge when discharging and vice versa!

Battery state indicator or voltmeter tells you how much voltage the batteries have. It should be the system's rated voltage at least and often a little bit more if the battery is in tip-top condition. Never forget under-volting electrical motors offends them! Your electrician can test the terminals with a simple multimeter and if they are found to be defective replace them.

Oil pressure gauges consist of two parts: the instrument head and the sender on the gearbox, engine or turbocharger. They become inaccurate or fail altogether, provided their indications are not a genuine mechanical fault; this must always be investigated first very thoroughly before suspecting the units. Malfunction may simply be due to dirty contacts.

Temperature gauges consist of a sender unit and instrument head and may fail completely or show deviation from the normal reading. Deviation from the normal reading must be checked to see that it is not a genuine fault in the cooling system. Genuine high temperatures may point to serious trouble and need instant investigation. Low temperatures may be thermostat failure in the open position. Occasionally you may find a gauge which consists of a metal bulb inserted and sealed into the cooling water passageway in the engine's casting and connected to an instrument head with a fine copper tube. The unit fails if the contents of the bulb and tube leak. It is simple to check this by removing the unit completely from the engine and dipping the bulb in hot water or holding a burning match temporarily under the bulb. Units often fail because of fractures caused by vibration, so put a coil in the tube between the sender and the head.

Tachometers may be either electrically operated or mechanical, with the drive taken from a shaft and led to the tachometer head via a flexible drive cable. The flexible drive cable should receive regular lubrication. Check for chafe; on no account should it be led through tight curves. The same remarks apply to engine control cables, although these are lubricated for life. Their exposed metal ends should receive regular corrosion proofing; check too that the outer sheath is not being mechanically damaged.

Fuel tank gauges of the electrical type are derived from the motor industry and consist of a sender unit and instrument head. The sender consists of a pivoting arm which changes the electrical resistance in the circuit as the fuel level drops. They are inaccurate since resistance bears no relationship at all to the shaped tanks generally employed on craft. However, they give a general indication and either fail completely or show an abnormal error which will draw attention. It may well be that the pivoting arm has jammed, necessitating opening up the fuel tank top to get at it. Always switch off before removing wires from the sender or a spark may explode the contents of a petrol tank.

Nearly all modern gauges are made as sealed units, and if you note condensation behind the glass, trouble may soon develop due to internal corrosion.

Batteries (Fig. 13)

These can be maintained quite easily and will certainly repay this effort by giving a more prolonged life and steady output voltage. They must be regularly inspected to see that the electrolyte level is maintained just above the plate tops (*never leave them uncovered*). Lead/acid batteries need plain distilled water for topping up or water from the melted ice of the refrigerator. Some genuine 'no maintenance' lead/acid batteries are slowly becoming available, but do read the manufacturer's literature to see that they really are what they say. 'Miracle' battery reconditioning solutions are a complete waste of money so don't be tempted.

If a battery is left discharged for long periods, sulphating on the plates takes place and the battery will slowly lose its charge, the rate being related to the ambient temperature. At 18°C (70°F) it will lose about 1 per cent of its charge each day. Now you can see why, even in winter temperatures, the battery should be at home in a trickle charger or in the electrician's care at the yard and charged every six to eight weeks. When a battery is receiving a charge, it gives off hydrogen and this is

WINTERISING

Charge battery once every six to eight weeks throughout the winter.

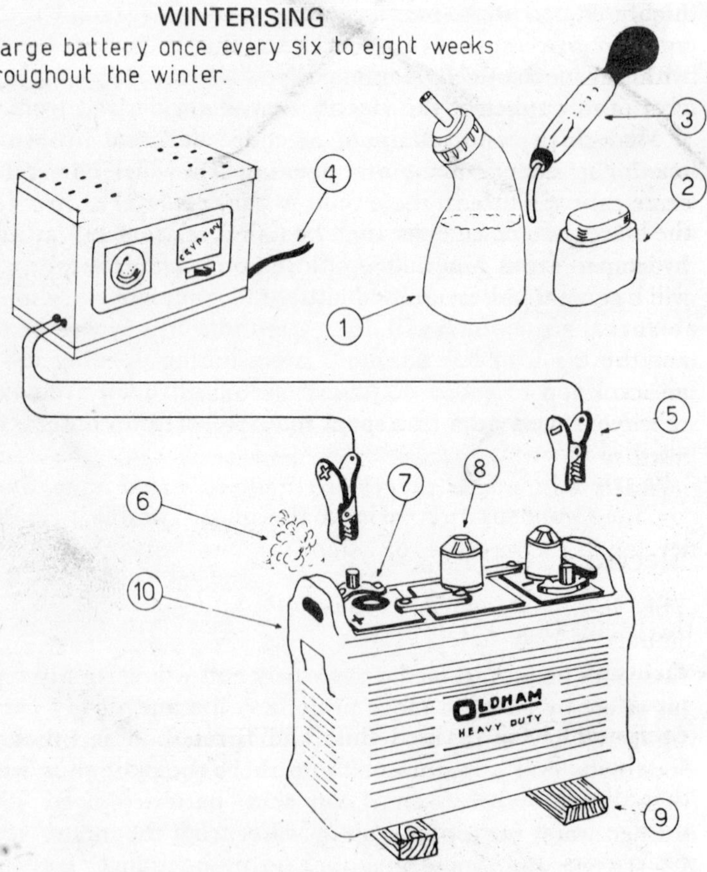

1. Only use distilled water from clean non-metallic vessel.
2. Smear terminal posts with petroleum jelly.
3. Use hydrometer for measuring the specific gravity of electrolyte.
4. Use correct voltage for both input and output.
5. Connect + to + and - to - with clips to battery terminal posts.
6. Explosive hydrogen given off during charging - NO SPARKS or FLAME.
7. Keep electrolyte topped up just above plates.
8. Use proper marine vent plugs if available.
9. Always isolate the battery when charging. Raise off damp floor.
10. Keep battery case, especially the top clean and dry.

Fig.13. Looking after the battery.

highly explosive. Battery terminals are subject to corrosion and should be kept scrupulously clean and regularly smeared with petroleum jelly. If spillage of electrolyte should occur, give a thorough wash down with clean water.

Modern yacht installations use a double bank of batteries, one for starting and one for services. Treat both banks to the same care and attention. If you don't have voltmeters, write to the battery manufacturer to get a specific gravity table; with a hydrometer and knowledge of the ambient temperature you will be able to test the state of charge.

Yachts may occasionally employ the alkaline type of battery and this is just as easy to maintain as the lead/acid variety. On no account contaminate an alkaline battery with a hydrometer previously used on a lead/acid one. Topping up is done with distilled water and the battery charged until the recommended specific gravity is reached.

Electronic Equipment

This has proliferated on yachts in recent years, causing embarrassment to yacht electrical systems and often to the yachtsman, who has neither the knowledge nor the facilities to repair and maintain it. The best manufacturers of electronic equipment have realised this, and firms such as Brookes & Gatehouse have gone to great lengths in their design to ensure that all their units can be easily removed for dry, warm winter storage, that they are sealed units using silica gel crystal desiccators and that the cable connectors are of the highest specification so that they will stand up to the corrosive environment in which they have to operate. We can learn something from their endeavours.

1. If you can remove electronic equipment to the safe keeping of your home, do so. Quite apart from winterisation, thieves may like to remove it to theirs!
2. Check desiccators and if the silica gel crystals are pink, gently warm them on the hot water tank or in a very low oven till they turn blue. *Never* place plastic bags over electronic gear on a boat unless the bag is sealed completely and contains a quantity of desiccator sufficient to remove water vapour. I have seen gear literally sweating with condensation!

3. Check cable connectors to see that soldered joints are properly made and intact. Only resin-cored solders are acceptable. Jointing should be smooth, well tinned during making and the solder melted directly onto the joint to provide a connection that does the job properly.
4. If equipment has to be left aboard during the winter, it must receive periodic attention. In this case, it is best to leave batteries aboard and trickle charge them *in situ*, then you can switch on integral electronic units and give them some use. Not much heat is generated in modern circuits but it is sufficient to dispel damp.
5. Before you suspect trouble in an electronic unit, check that a fuse has not blown. Some installers have a nasty habit of fitting 'in line' hot line (+) fuses which they then proceed to hide behind panelling or in an equally awkward place where it will generate a good game of hide and seek. The best practice is to wire each unit direct to a distribution board with 'Lupus' type circuit breakers matched to the maker's power requirement, otherwise instal a fuse at the unit itself so that it is accessible. Open fuses deteriorate with age, so they can blow at a lower value than normal. Check with manufacturers about the correct rating for fuses supplying their units, and carry spares.
6. Connectors of the co-axial type should have plastic plugs inserted in them during lay-up to keep out dirt.
7. Units using internal batteries *must be removed* during winterisation or they could do serious damage as they disintegrate. The cost of new batteries each season is a small price to pay for reliability and safety.
8. Never pull plugs or transducers out by their connecting wire or wires may break internally.
9. Never tolerate voltage drop through long cables, and check that your battery amp/hours are sufficient to cope with new gear.

Logs and speedometers

The 'sender' heads may be inside the boat (doppler types) or outside (impeller or pitot types). Fouling is a serious matter for the latter and hence the great advantage of having valve housings which allow them to be withdrawn for cleaning. Use only a detergent solution for the cleaning of any underwater parts, using a toothbrush. Impellers should be examined for mechanical damage and excessive play in bearings. Some units only need a new impeller, while in others the whole unit has to be replaced. Both logs and depth sounders on yachts often employ changeover switches so that underwater units work on either tack. It is unusual for them to fail together, so one can be checked against the other. Check that weed deflectors are not damaged and are prefectly in line with the impeller.

Depth sounders

Much of the foregoing applies to these units but pay special attention to the face of the underwater transducer unit. It must *never* be contaminated with grease, paint, anti-fouling or any other chemical. Its face is sensitive and even an abrasive cleaner will damage it. Use only a soft rag with detergent for cleaning it.

Skin fitting valves mentioned here in connection with the above two instruments, but equally applicable to intakes for engine cooling water, head valves, and exhaust skin fitting valves. A lanolin waterproof-type grease is highly suitable for all metal skin fittings to keep them working smoothly. Tapered valves such as the 'Blake' pattern used on their heads can be reground by using a valve grinding paste on their surfaces and slowly rotating the handle until even contact is shown over the whole face of the valve; then thoroughly remove all paste, grease and reassemble. Silicone greases are happier where valves have neoprene rubber seals, as in transducer housings. I like to disconnect all skin fittings and service them at lay-up time and then leave them open so that some low down ventilation is provided during the winter. This is especially welcome in any yacht bilge area. Keep an eye on the wall thickness of any skin fitting as they can be eaten away and failure could be disastrous. Note particularly where water flows and impinges for that is the danger spot. I regularly treat water intakes and exhaust fittings with an epoxy-based paint system which works excellently.

Wind direction and speed indicators

Could you put any instrument in a worse location than on the top of a mast? The real weakness is in the cable connections between the sender unit and the instrument head. Connectors have to be perfectly sealed and the wire protected from chafe.

Try to fit rubber grommets where the cable enters an aluminium mast. Never use aluminium connectors onto copper wire in the marine environment: they hate each other and the aluminium will seize and disintegrate within weeks. The weight of the mast wire must be taken at a head grommet and not by a connector at the top of the mast.

Aerials and earths

These play a vital role in helping various electronic gear function properly. Maintain both regularly as they are extremely susceptible to corrosion: the earth because it is connected through the bilges to a ground plate and the aerial because it is open to all weather, either on the mast or high up on a cabin top. Inspect for chafe and mechanical damage and do some clipping to keep the earth out of bilge water.

Auto pilots

These consist of a magnetic or wind direction sensor, a control unit which allows manual correction to course setting, a relay which transmits this information, and a mechanical drive which applies the course to the rudder. Each part of the whole should receive periodic maintenance. The electronic part is beyond the amateur but, again, look for well maintained connections, proper power supply, and keep all parts dry and clean both in and out of season. Electric motors are often utilised for working either a chain drive or a hydraulic pump for moving rudders. These motors should be kept clean and serviced in accordance with the manufacturer's instructions. Note that a gearbox reduction is often utilised, and this may need periodic servicing with the correct grade lubricant. Drive chains and sprockets must receive regular lubrication with chain lubricant. Occasionally remove chains completely and soak off dirt in a paraffin bath, drain, dry and relubricate. Carry spare chain links.

Chapter 8
GENERAL YACHT EQUIPMENT

The modern yacht has become much more sophisticated in the range of equipment carried because most of us like to try and achieve the same standard of comfort (or pretty near it!) that we have at home. This does mean we have a lot more to go wrong unless we see that the whole lot is properly maintained. A good deal of this equipment can go seriously wrong and endanger both the boat and your life, so maintenance is a vital duty that will be accepted by any proper seaman. I head the list of equipment with the fire fighting appliances. Only when these are actually being serviced should the yacht be without them.

Fire Equipment

This depends on pressure from gases to eject the fire fighting medium from the extinguisher. It may be carbon dioxide gas contained in a small cylinder under high pressure or perhaps nitrogen as used to drive out BCF (Bromodichloromethane) in that type of extinguisher. Provided you follow the maker's instruction leaflet carefully, it is a simple matter to service most makes of dry powder extinguisher which utilises a small CO_2 cartridge and a packet of replacement powder. These cartridges can lose their contents, which gradually leak out, but they are stamped with their total 'full' weight and they can be check-weighed. A similar cylinder is often used in soda syphons and on automatic inflation lifejackets, and the same test can be applied. Dry powders tend to settle and can clog. A monthly 'shake up' is advisable if packing is to be avoided.

All other types of extinguisher should have an agency servicing as there is no way of testing if all is well with the contents. It is unfortunate that many yachts carry small hand extinguishers which are quite unsuitable for marine operations. The containers corrode quickly and their pressurising contents leak so that they are utterly useless after a very short time. Check if you are living in a fool's paradise! I suggest it would be a valuable lesson for the skipper to take the yacht's extinguisher ashore and try it out on a small fire.

Cooking Stoves

Three basic types are found on yachts – the alcohol stove, the paraffin (kerosene) and the LPG (liquid petroleum gas). Each type of fuel has its own following who swear that the variety they choose is safer and better in every way than the other two types. The fact is, although they have their virtues, they are all capable of setting both you and your yacht on fire unless they are used correctly and maintained in perfect order.

Paraffin and alcohol stoves

There are two distinctive sections to maintain on both paraffin and alcohol stoves. These are the fuel storage part, which is pressurised by means of a pump, and the burner.

The storage tank must be kept scrupulously clean and spillage dealt with immediately. Inspect the tank and piping for leaks, usually just weeping but nevertheless intolerable from the point of view of safety.

The pump will be a simple piston type with a sealing washer that traps air in the barrel and, as it is forced down, pushes it into the tank via a check valve. The valve allows air to enter but the air pressure in the tank forces it back onto its seating to seal the tank after the delivery stroke. Both parts can cause trouble.

The piston washer may occasionally be sparingly oiled to keep it supple, but on no account must excess oil be used; it is better to carry spare pump washers.

The check valve must be cleaned if pressure is constantly falling or the tank will not take pressure at all. Check the pressure filling cap, which also carries a sealing washer, and the pressure gauge when one is fitted to the tank, as these can leak.

The burner, as well as producing the flame for the stove, has two other functions. The first is a means of vapourising the fuel as it comes from the tank to the burner head and the second is to control that amount of fuel so that you get the right size flame. In my opinion, vapourising is the big drawback to these stoves as it takes some time for a heater flame to vapourise the fuel at the burner head, and if the allotted time is not allowed a dirty flame, which helps gum up the fine burner nozzle, will be the result. Once you are able to judge the pre-heating phase well this problem can be avoided, but in any case dirty burning will inevitably occur and one must know how to clean the burner jet.

Some jets require a simple pricker consisting of a fine wire mounted on a short tin-plate holder. These are usually found at the critical moment rusted to hell in the bilges. Carry spares and keep them in a small tobacco tin with a rust-inhibiting paper in it. In the same tin carry spare burners and the correct tool for removing and replacing them. Prickers should be used once a day when stoves are in use to keep the jet clean. Some stoves have self-pricking burners. They are very worth-while for obvious reasons, although they are more mechanically complicated and the maker's directions must be followed if they are to be maintained correctly.

Basically, the parts that go wrong are the needle point, which wears, and the spindle packing, which leaks. The burner control wheel must always work smoothly as most makers insist that after the vapourising period the valve must be opened only slowly and for quite a small amount. A jerky valve could just send a jet of unvapourised fuel right up to the deckhead! The yellow, smoky, weak or unbalanced flame is a sure indicator that some part of the system is not functioning correctly, so always keep the stove's instruction manual to hand so that an exact diagnosis can be made.

One last word: if you carry different types of fuel aboard, carry them in very distinctive labelled cans so that there can be no doubt that the outboard's petrol does not find its way into the cooker, with explosive results!

LPG stoves

LPG is often known under various other names, including Calor Gas, Butane or Propane. It is heavier than air so that if a leak occurs it falls into the bilges and builds up till it reaches to the height where you strike the fatal match and there is no further need for you to read books about boating! Reference is made in Chapter 10 to testing procedures, and this must be done if there is a slightest suspicion of a leak.

Calor has a nasty musty smell put into it, but I have been amazed (and frightened!) when I have found really serious leaks on yachts and the owner had no suspicion that anything was wrong. Every time a gas bottle is disconnected, the plastic sealing cap should be replaced as well as the main valve turned off. The flexible connection has a sealing washer and that, too, must be replaced each time. The gas compartment must have wide gas drains in the bottom so that any small escape of gas caused when changing bottles can drop safely over the side of the yacht. Clean these drains regularly and wash the compartment out so that debris can never clog them.

Never use other than the manufacturer's own make of gas connecting equipment. Flexible armoured hoses and special flexible gas piping is specially made to withstand the gas. Other pipes will rapidly fail and be an immense danger. Calor Gas will advise freely on the use of their products and have excellent installation and safety leaflets available.

At the risk of heaping fires of coal on my head, I will say that I am against having too great a faith in gas detecting equipment. There are gas sniffers which tell you if there is gas in the bilge, and there are sniffers which tell you if gas is there and turn off the gas for you at the gas bottle. There is not a unit which does all this and empties the offending gas out! Your nose is the best gas detector there is, being independent of batteries, wires, complicated physics and integrated circuits. If you insist on investing money, why not get a really good fan - up to the mining safety standards of being spark- and flame-proof - so that this heavy gas actually can be safely moved from the bilges? A.K. Fans make Airmax Gasextractor units and centrifugal fans which meet Lloyds and Board of Trade requirements for units that are entirely safe to handle explosive gas mixtures.

Ventilation

This is a hobbyhorse of mine. I have no doubt at all that a great number of problems are caused or accentuated by the fact that the vast majority of yachts are appallingly badly ventilated.

Rot in woods is aided by lack of ventilation, but some yachtsmen think that because the boat is made of GRP why worry about rot? They don't bother to think of the needs of the next most expensive part of the boat, the engine. So long as the smelly, noisy thing is shut away out of sight they simply could not care less about it, until perhaps it is wanted in a real emergency when it won't work anyway because of neglect. The cold metal of the engine always provides a good surface for condensation to form. You can open up many an engine hatch and see the beads of corroding sweat eating the unit away and, incidentally, saying much of the character of the owner. We are equally familiar with condensation in cabins, in bilges and the sickly smell that so many yachts seem to have by the time you reach them at the weekend. Any of these symptoms really should be dealt with. At winterising time it is even more essential to provide excellent ventilation so that every part of the boat can have moving air through it.

1. Look into means of mechanical ventilation if your battery capacity will allow this. Seek professional advice, for the 'toy' ventilators so often sold to the yachtsman are almost worthless in their ability to get air really moving through the lower part of the hull. A.K. Fans give an excellent advisory service.
2. Check that there are static ventilators in each enclosed section of the boat and that some of the air is led down to bilge level.
3. Louvred doors look attractive and are very efficient, keeping rain out and letting air through.
4. Metal and plastic ventilators are plentiful and can look aesthetically pleasing if chosen carefully. Use them in the bottom of cupboards, on top of doors, on the front of lockers, and to ventilate any otherwise totally enclosed space, such as

in parts of panelling.
5. Check that winter covers allow a full circulation of air.
6. If you are near an electricity supply, a small tubular heater will keep damp at bay and stop moisture content of wood and panelling from rising too high. I would certainly recommend that this is done only when you visit the yacht; it can be quite a pleasure if you choose one of those bright, breezy winter days to go down and check over things.

Heating Installations

These are now common on even small craft and they need attention if they are to function correctly and not be a danger. There is, in fact, extreme danger to life if any heater burns up the oxygen in a cabin space. Leaks of carbon monoxide from a faulty engine exhaust or heater flue will kill.

The main item to check is that on solid fuel stoves using a flue it is gas tight and not suffering from blockage or dangerous corrosion. Corrosion is often accentuated because so much water vapour is produced when carbonaceous fuels are burned. Solid fuel stoves often have sealing strips to prevent the escape of combustion products and these must be maintained. Winterising includes removing fuels from any type of stove and cleaning down.

Asbestos is now regarded as a dangerous product if it is dusting and flaking. If fire-protective panelling is in this dangerous condition; replace it with a safe substitute such as Turner-Newall 'Ferroform 90', which does exactly the same job as the old asbestos sheet.

Some diesel burning heaters such as the 'Webasto', 'Eberspächer' and LPG gas 'Remotron' heaters have ignition plugs which are treated exactly the same as spark plugs for cleaning and gapping. Look for weeping on liquid fuel pipes and test gas pipes with liquid soap, as no leak of any kind can be tolerated.

Finally, check that the air intake to any appliance is free and clean. For solid fuel stoves this might simply be air holes in the sole of the cabin or in other units ducting from outside the boat. The remarks on paraffin pressure stoves are generally applicable for the maintenance of paraffin pressure heaters.

Marine Heads

At the time of writing there are at least forty types of marine head on the world market and I cannot help but think that someone, somewhere, takes fiendish delight in designing so many. There are already so many different models installed on boats that this causes great confusion when spare parts are needed, unless the owner knows the manufacturer's address, the model of the head and, if possible, the year of manufacture. I cannot hope to mention every model available, but I can advise owners wishing to maintain the heads on their boats to write to the manufacturer for servicing and spares leaflets.

Anti-pollution legislation now in force in the USA and under consideration by European countries has prompted the development of yacht toilet systems which either contain the effluent or make it safe for discharge.

Broadly speaking, there are two basic types of head: the sea-toilet which draws its flushing water from the sea and discharges effluent (if allowed) back there or into a holding tank, and the re-circulating toilet (Fig. 14), like the Thetford 'Porta Potti 44', which contains its own flushing water inhibited with a chemical that renders effluent less offensive. This can be used as a fully portable unit or connected to a deck pump outlet or holding tank connection, and can be built into the boat and emptied out at the dock side. Some units re-circulate the same water after chemical treatment and filtration in a self-contained holding tank. Both types depend on a variety of pumps to obtain a flushing action of fresh/sea water and to discharge the effluent. The pumps may be either hand or electrically operated. The problem of so many different head types may be simplified by saying that troubles can usually be pinned down to four main parts of the toilet system.

Valves on inlet and discharge sections

Some systems have gunmetal valves of the tapered plug type. The proper seating and smooth working of this type is essential. After washing to clear loose debris from the body of the valve in the hull of the boat, remove the tapered plug and smear a fine grinding paste over the working faces. Insert the plug in the body and rotate back and forth to grind the two

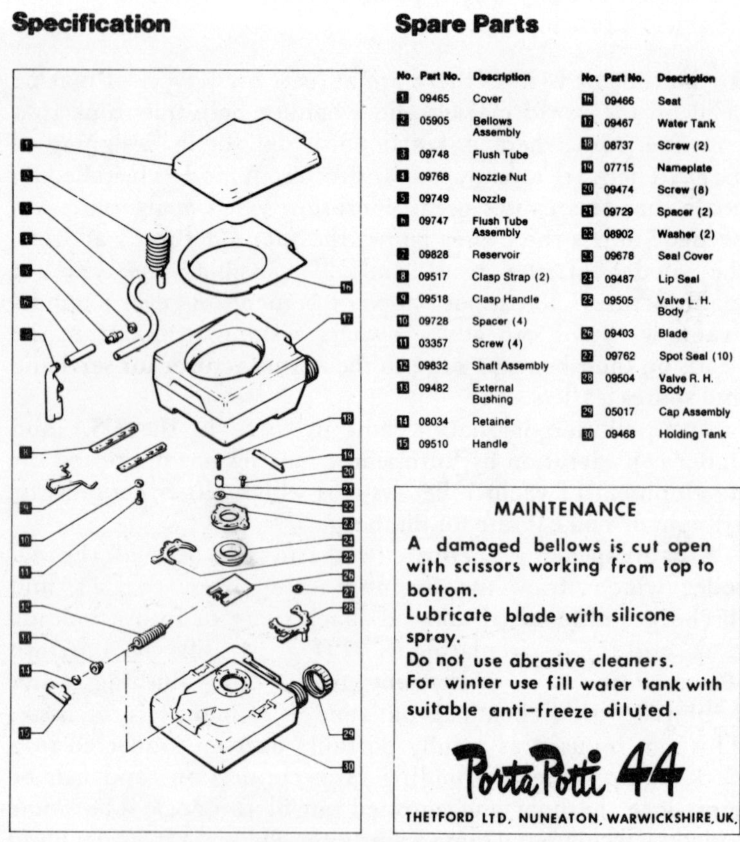

Specification

Spare Parts

No.	Part No.	Description
1	09465	Cover
2	05905	Bellows Assembly
3	09748	Flush Tube
4	09768	Nozzle Nut
5	09749	Nozzle
6	09747	Flush Tube Assembly
7	09828	Reservoir
8	09517	Clasp Strap (2)
9	09518	Clasp Handle
10	09728	Spacer (4)
11	03357	Screw (4)
12	09832	Shaft Assembly
13	09482	External Bushing
14	08034	Retainer
15	09510	Handle
16	09466	Seat
17	09467	Water Tank
18	08737	Screw (2)
19	07715	Nameplate
20	09474	Screw (8)
21	09729	Spacer (2)
22	08902	Washer (2)
23	09678	Seal Cover
24	09487	Lip Seal
25	09505	Valve L. H. Body
26	09403	Blade
27	09762	Spot Seal (10)
28	09504	Valve R. H. Body
29	05017	Cap Assembly
30	09468	Holding Tank

Fig.14. Porta Potti 44 Head

surfaces perfectly together. Flush away every trace of grinding paste, smear lanolin grease on both parts and reassemble the unit. The valve should then work very smoothly and there should be no weeps on re-launching. Check this!

Ball valves are quite often found on systems on the inlet when the toilet is at a high level. The ball (sometimes weighted) drops by gravity onto a seating aided by the weight of fluid above it. It seals onto the seating, preventing back flow. Check that the seating is good and the ball is in good condition. If the ball is worn or distorted, renew it. A ball valve of this type is often used in the effluent discharge pump of sea-toilets such as the 'Baby' shown in more detail in Fig. 15.

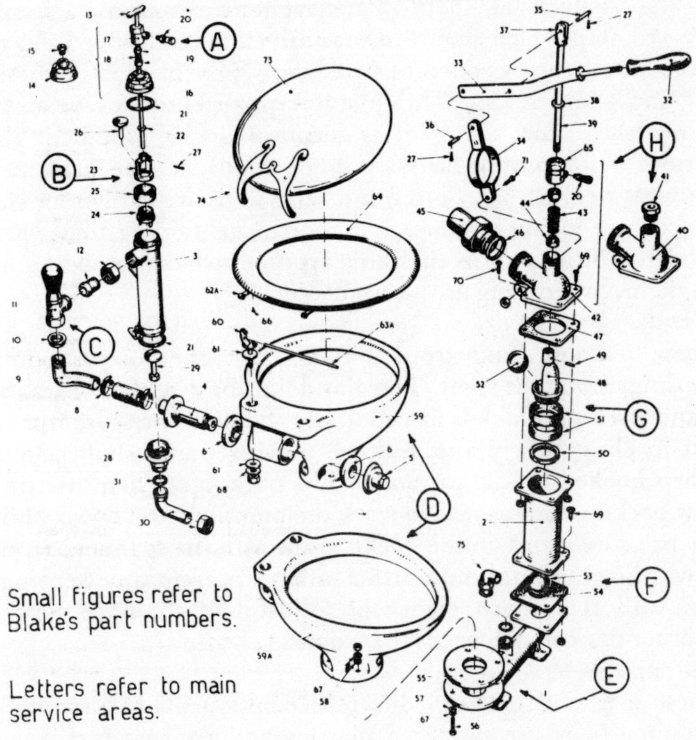

A. Flushing water pump gland. Check packing or the action of self adjusting glands. (15, 17, 18, 19, 20.).
B. Check upper valve (26) and rubber bucket (25) for seating and seal. Also lower valve (29).
C. Wheel control valve must close fully.
D. Keep pan clean but do not use domestic toilet cleaners. Oil based products will damage rubber parts.
E. Joint on pan base (55) must not weep.
F. Lower cylinder joint (54) forms valve that naval brass ball must seat on properly (53).
G. Discharge pump washers (51) must be good fit in discharge cylinder (2).
H Glands (41, 65) must be checked.

Blakes carry full service kits of perishable parts.

Fig. 15 Blake 'Baby' Marine Head

'Flap' valves, as their name suggests, contain a simple pivoted flap which opens in one direction, allowing fluid to pass, but as the direction of stroke or weight of fluid changes, the flap is forced shut. With metal flaps, attention to the hinge is necessary and a rub of waterproof grease will help the action. Some pumps have a rubber or plastic flap held with stainless steel screws. Both screws and flaps are easily renewed if they are giving trouble. It is worth mentioning that when servicing **bilge pumps** the same types of valves may be found on them, so servicing advice applies equally.

Glands

These prevent fluid from leaking past the top of pump housings along the shaft. The gland may be a rubber or waxed gland packing which is forced under the slight pressure from a nut to cling closely and seal the moving pump shaft. Use a sharp hooked needle to remove old packing. When inserting new packing, it is as well to work the pump up and down while the pressure is put on the packing nut with the spanner. Screw down the gland nut only sufficiently to prevent any weeping. You will then have plenty of adjustment to make before another packing job needs to be done.

Seals and joints

These are used between different components of sanitation systems. They are made of plastics and rubbers of various kinds. They have to be water-tight and sometimes gas-tight. The wrong kinds of cleaning chemicals can damage them and some fail through old-age hardening. Most toilet manufacturers provide service kits which contain full sets of perishable parts, and these are so reasonably priced that it is hardly ever worth carrying various thicknesses of sheet rubber and plastic in order to cut your own. Sliding seals on some re-circulating units can be lubricated with silicone-based oils if their action becomes stiff.

Pumps

Although we are really discussing pumps in relation to the marine head, if we understand the basic working principles this knowledge will be equally applicable to pumps of identical type which are used for such diverse applications as fresh water, bilge, fuel and galley pumps. Three basic types of pump are shown in Fig. 16 and Fig. 17. Note that the basic

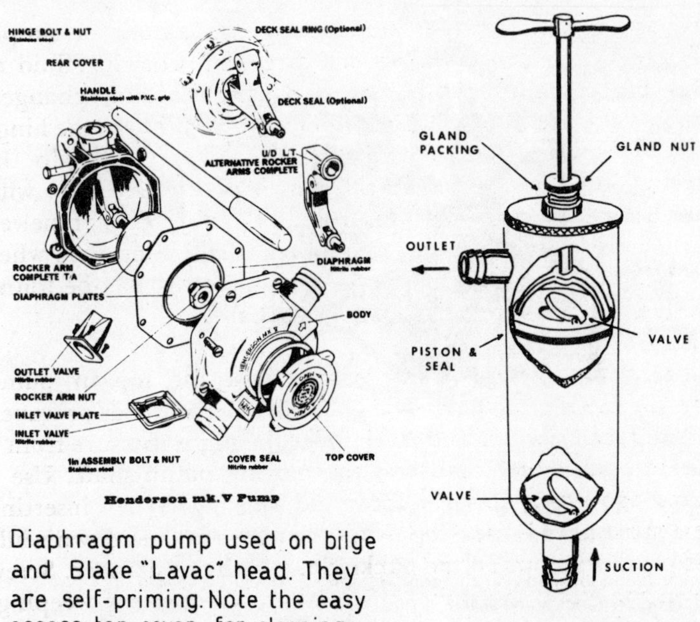

Diaphragm pump used on bilge and Blake "Lavac" head. They are self-priming. Note the easy access top cover for cleaning.

Lift Pump

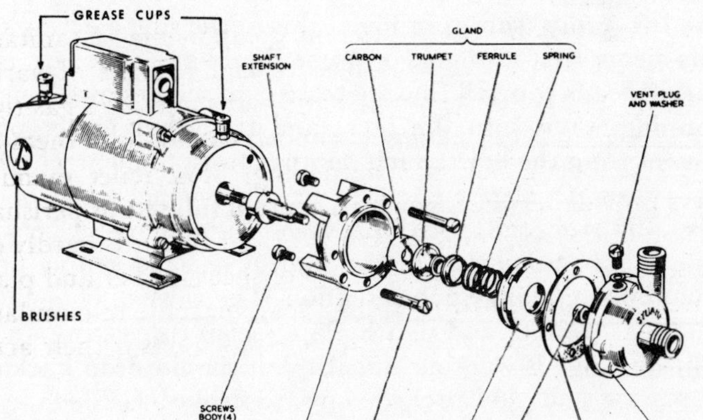

Centrifugal pump by Stuart Turner. Not self-priming so needs either drowned suction or footvalve.

Fig.16. Types of Marine Pump

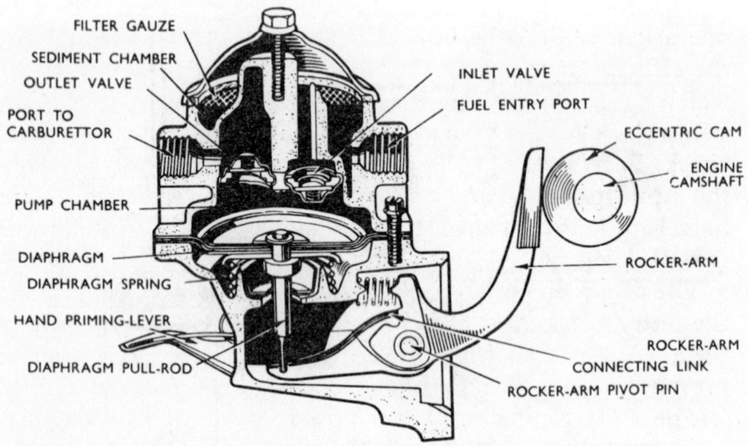

Fig. 17. A.C.-Delco Fuel Lift Pump
Used on both petrol and diesel engines to supply fuel to either a carburettor or diesel injection pump. The filter gauze can be kept clean but although spares kits are available and inexpensive, the complete pump should be carried on a yacht since servicing demands some skill.

working principle of the A.C.-Delco fuel lift pump is related to the Henderson diaphragm pump.

The lift pump (shown in Fig. 16) is of the single acting type. This means that it pumps only one liquid at a time. On many marine heads you will find there are two such pumps – one for pumping water into the bowl and the other for emptying effluent from the bowl. Such pumps consist of a barrel, piston and valves. One part likely to need servicing is the bottom valve (flap or ball), sticking open with debris. Check the strainer on the outside of the hull on a head supply or the strum box on a bilge pump suction. The valve may be hinged metal or a rubber and plastic flap. Clean the seating and see that the hinge is working smoothly: it should drop back onto the seating smoothly after the upward stroke has filled the barrel with water. The next downward stroke should see a transfer of the water in the barrel into the top as it is forced past the valve in the piston. The next upward stroke sees the water at the top forced out (the piston valve seating so that liquid cannot fall down into the lower part of the barrel) and the new lot of water sucked into the lower section.

On some heads you will find one pump which performs both operations – filling the bowl with flushing water and emptying the effluent at the same time. This is a double acting pump which has a solid piston with no valve in it. The top half of the pump has a twin valve system as has the bottom – four valves to check. Each stroke of the pump causes alternate action; thus the upward stroke causes suction in the lower part of the barrel while the downward stroke causes suction in the upper part of the barrel.

The piston on both types of lift pump must be a good fit and the piston seals must be renewed if there is any leakage past them. A gland on the piston shaft may need servicing to prevent liquid carried in the barrel from oozing up the handle.

The winterising of any type of pump demands that no water is left in it to freeze and burst the barrel or damage the valves.

The diaphragm pump has become increasingly popular in recent years, performing just about every function needed on the modern yacht. The Henderson MK5 (illustrated in Fig. 16) is used on the Blake 'Lavac' marine head as well as for bilge pumping, fresh water and fuel transfer.

The flexing of the diaphragm is basically the same principle as that employed on the A.C.-Delco fuel lift pump shown in Fig. 17. (This was the pump I referred to in Fig. 11 which plays such an important part in pumping the fuel supply to diesel and petrol engines from the fuel tank.) There are two valves on either side of a pump chamber and a rubber flexible diaphragm which, when moved back and forth by means of either manual power or a cam being driven from the engine or electric motor, alternately increases and decreases the volume in the pump chamber. This induces first suction via the inlet valve and then on the opposite stroke compression, which first closes the inlet valve then, as it increases, forces the liquid being pumped out through the outlet valve. The only parts to go wrong are the two valves and the diaphragm. The valves can stick or fracture and the diaphragm can rupture.

On heads there can be a problem when under pumping allows solids to jam in one of the valves – the pump will not then function. The Henderson MK5 now being used on 'Lavac' heads overcomes this problem neatly with a front access cap which enables the valves to be reached easily. When servicing this unit (Fig. 18) you must take care to ensure the siphon break valve at the top of the inlet water pipe loop is kept clean. A blocked valve here will cause the boat to flood as water will then be continuously siphoned into the boat!

Although the A.C.-Delco pump is similar and full service kits are available at small cost, their servicing is specialised, needing care, cleanliness and the proper service manual; it is far easier to take these small pumps into a service depot. If you think you might have one break down while you are at sea, carry a complete spare pump unit – I'd hate to think of putting one together in a Force eight!

Centrifugal pumps are not found on head applications but are more usually associated with electric pumps for fresh water supply, for circulating fresh water cooling on marine engines, for domestic water systems, pumping hot or cold water supplies or central heating circulation. This type of pump is, unlike all the others so far mentioned, not self priming. This means that when the pump is started it is unable to suck up water by itself but must be 'primed' or full of water before it starts. It always needs a 'drowned suction'. On the engine, the pump is primed simply by keeping the water topped up in the header tank. Domestic supplies may have a drowned suction simply by installing the inlet to the pump below the level of the water tank. Where this type of pump is used above the level of the tank, a foot valve is employed. This ensures that the pipe up to the pump inlet is always kept full by means of a one-way valve. If there is the slightest leak in this valve the water drains down back to the tank, the 'head' of water is lost and the pump will not function. This type of pump is, for the same reason, also susceptible to air leaks into connecting piping and to air locks on the suction side. Points to watch in centrifugal pump maintenance are as follows.

1. Keep suction pipes well clamped and primed. In winterisation, when the water system and pump must be completely emptied to prevent frost damage, take the opportunity offered to inspect foot valves.
2. Leaking from the gland along the shaft must never be tolerated or severe damage will be done by shorting the motor. Inspect glands regularly.
3. Check vent plugs and bleed the system when fitting-out

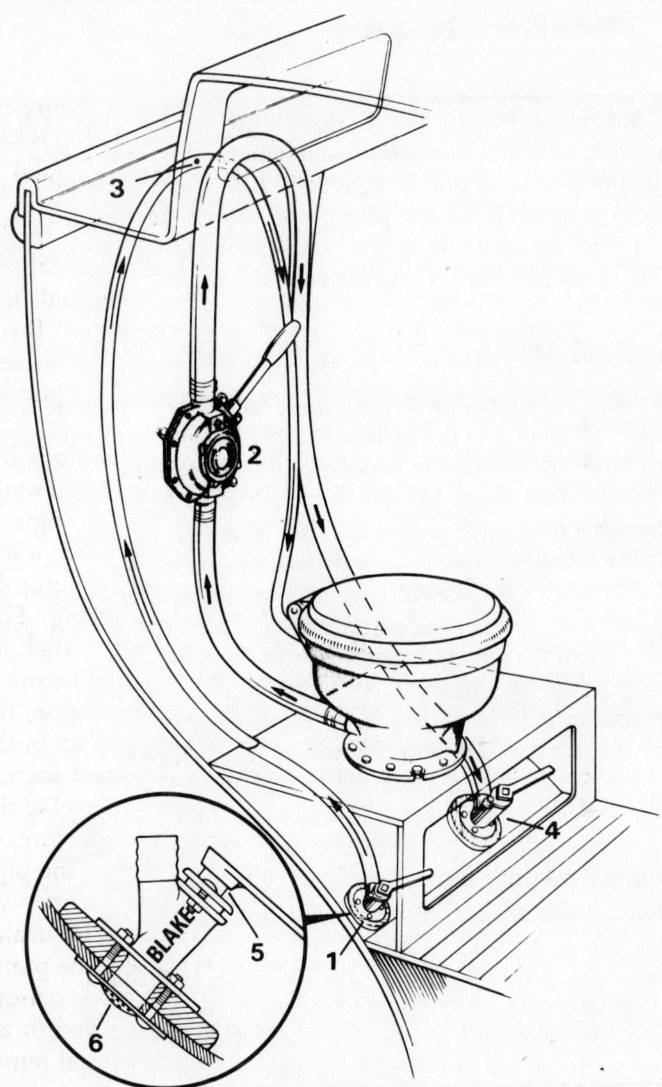

Fig. 18. Service Points on Blake 'Lavac' Marine Head

1. Inlet seacock. Clean strainer (6) from the outside and remove debris internally by removing taper plug valve (5) on the inside. Both inlet and discharge seacocks should be ground in with water-based valve grinding paste. Every trace of this must be removed and the plugs lubricated with lanolin grease before re-assembly.
2. Henderson diaphragm pump. See Fig. 16 for service parts.
3. Air Bleed Valve. Vital to keep this clean as it breaks the vacuum in the flushing water pipe after pumping stops. It will flood your boat unless this valve is in working order.
4. Discharge seacock. See (1) for servicing.

after winterisation. In installations using a foot valve, fill the inlet pipe between the valve and where this joints onto the pump body with water so that it is full and the rotor of the pump is primed. Start the pump and loosen the bleed screw so that liquid without air is ejected. Then, when the system is fully primed and bled, close the vent screw.

Electrical Motors

I have already mentioned these in connection with centrifugal pumps, but they also occur in a multiplicity of applications on board modern yachts. On small yachts we are likely to find two kinds. The first type, inherited from the motor industry, are inexpensive and have a limited life. They are found on light pumping duties, low-cost ventilating units and low-cost windscreen wipers. They are factory-sealed and when they are worn out they are simply replaced with a boxed factory unit. Their minimal cadmium plating should be protected with a spot of paint to ensure they don't rust up quickly in an environment for which they were not designed.

The more expensive motors have a much longer life and do need some regular maintenance. They are used on head pumps, larger pressurised water systems, deck winches, bilge pumps, auto-pilot drives and superior ventilating systems and, of course, engine starter motors. On them you will find 'brushes' made of carbon and held onto the commutator by means of a spring. The carbon is worn away by the commutator rotation and the spring keeps a constant pressure as this progressive wear takes place. Sometimes the spring will weaken with age and because of wear and this weakness, the proper contact by the brush is not made. Although it is normal for some small blue arcing to occur on the commutator at the brushes, red arcing means that servicing is most necessary. Always carry the maker's specification replacement brushes. Their exact fit in the brush chamber and the precise spring length to produce the brush pressure are vital statistics.

Remove debris from the commutator by the use of trichloroethylene (dangerous if not used in accordance with packer's instructions). When cleaned, look to see that no ridges have been developed by wear. If worn, it may need 'skimming' in a lathe or replacing. The new brushes must take up the shape of the commutator exactly so that the whole of their contact surface really is in contact with it. Although it is unusual for the shaped end of the brush not to fit the commutator's curve, this can in emergency be obtained by wrapping a fine abrasive paper around the commutator and inserting the brush into contact with it so that rotation on the paper shapes up the end of the brush. Ensure that debris does not fall into the motor and clean off thoroughly before re-assembly.

Most damage is done to electric motors by under-volting. The power consumption is exceedingly high at the start compared to that needed once rotation has commenced. Check that long cable runs have not robbed the motor of its much needed voltage. Also check that fuses for the motor are properly rated to cope with the initial starting surge of power. These larger motors often have oiling or greasing points that need occasional attention - use the manufacturer's recommended oil or grease. On no account over-lubricate as this can run into the motor and damage the windings by rotting the insulation. Some aerosol inhibitors can be safely used to protect electric motors from damp and corrosion.

Steering Gear

This may be direct via a tiller, which needs little maintenance except inspection of metal parts for fatigue cracks, or be of a mechanical type which needs both regular inspection and maintenance. The types I've included here are cable linked systems, mechanical systems using bevel boxes and torque tubes, and hydraulic steering gear.

Cable linked systems - using a wheel, pulley blocks and wire cables

Check that cables are not wearing through: signs to look for are single strand breaks, especially where the cable passes round blocks. Do not test with bare hands as this can end in nasty spiking. Plain wire cables of either galvanised or stainless steel variety are given a longer life if their strands work with a lanolin grease lubrication, wiped on with a rag. Pulley blocks and sliders on the tiller steering arm must be free running. On some installations, half-hooded leads will be used where the steering cables emerge from beneath the deck to the tiller arm above deck. It is at these leads that chafe on the wires is most likely to ruin them.

Mechanical systems

These, like the excellent Mathway steering gear, need very little maintenance, provided bevel boxes and torque tubes are kept free of corrosion with one of the high-performance paint systems. Oil or grease, according to type, is put in the bevel boxes at the factory and could in unusual circumstances leak from an oil seal. This is, however, most unlikely, but you should give the splined universal joints a shot of grease on the grease nipples provided. Check that ball joints found at the ends of tie rods and drag links are properly adjusted, that split pins are in position and that they are fully greased regularly. A well-looked-after system really will last a lifetime.

Hydraulic steering

This needs regular inspection for leaks and topping up of the hydraulic oil reservoir. A leak is a very serious matter and may occur on seals on the transmitter, actuator or at connections on the pipe system. Dirt *must* be kept out of the system, and while inspecting for leaks it is always worth-while cleaning all parts down with a clean duster. Seals of synthetic rubber and any flexible piping do deteriorate with age, so spares should be carried. The service manual should tell you how to bleed air from a newly repaired system that has been refilled. Always use the maker's recommended hydraulic fluid as specifications do differ.

Chapter 9
LAYING-UP PROCEDURES

Afloat

1. Check all systems and make notes for repairs needed.
2. Winterise engine.
3. Removal and stowage of items that could be damaged when craning out.
4. Flushing of holding and sanitation tanks.

Ashore

1. Inspection of hull below the waterline. Touching-up to prevent weather attack (frost and water).
2. Mast, rigging and sails. Removal, maintenance.
3. Winterise outboard motor.
4. Batteries and electrical system.
5. Toilet compartment.
6. Fresh water system.
7. Galley.
8. Safety equipment.
9. Hull, topsides and deck equipment.
10. Winter covers, cradles and legs.
11. Security and insurance.
12. Miscellaneous items.

If I were to suggest a motto for the prudent yachtsman it would be 'Before - not after', for it is always better and less expensive to take preventative measures and do repairs than to neglect and then have to effect a cure. Many of the items in the above lay-up programme are dealt with specifically in the preceding chapters. It is worth expanding on some of the points so that you have a clear idea for the reasons behind suggested procedures.

In winter, our chief enemies are damp atmosphere, condensation and frost. Relatively warm air in autumn condenses onto relatively cold surfaces: bare areas of a GRP hull and the cold engine castings are places that will suffer most. Too often we cover our boats so well that even when there is a breeze the air lies dank in most of the hull. Sometimes, when the weather is bad, we get that feeling of wanting to get the lay-up job done quickly and then forget about her until the first twitches of spring. Nothing could be worse for a boat than damp and neglect. Let's look in more detail at the items listed above.

Afloat

1. A list of all the jobs you were going to do all summer and containing all the items that have been on the blink will serve as a conscience prodder. The same list will enable you to get orders for replacement parts in early to the chandler or see new equipment at the boat shows which take place in the closed season. A list enables this to be done at a leisurely pace and get delivery in plenty of time so that energy and nerves are not frayed when spring arrives but the spares don't.
2. Engine winterising is best done afloat for inboard engines or out-drive power units. Run the engine with its normal supply of cooling water till the oil is well up to temperature, then empty it, with all its filth and sludge, and change the oil filters. Drain the gearbox and reduction gear at the same time, immediately after a run; change any gearbox oil filter too. With diesel-inhibiting oils in the fuel and lubrication systems, run the engine up to working temperature to coat all internal surfaces of the fuel system, pumps/injectors with the oil. Petrol engines use only the lubricating system inhibiting oils, but should have spark plugs removed and about one tablespoonful of oil placed in each cylinder. Then turn over the engine, preferably by hand, to coat the cylinder walls with the oil. If you have to use the electric starter motor to turn over

the engine, for goodness sake isolate the high tension leads so that they don't spark around, and put a rag over the plug holes or you will have engine oil thrown all over the place.

The rest of the winterisation programme for the engine accessories is dealt with in Chapter 6.

I like to complete winterisation of the engine while afloat, but this means you have to have her towed to the hauling-out crane or slip. If you need to motor to the hauling-out place, you can carry out the lubricating procedures but not the cooling water system ones. In this case, do the water system while it is still warm immediately after the lift-out. The warmth in the castings will then dry out internal surfaces if you are to drain them completely.

On engines with indirect cooling, some yachtsmen prefer to leave the fresh water system 'wet', using a recommended anti-freeze to protect the unit from frost damage. This method has the advantage that on some engines it is easier to dose with anti-freeze than to get every drop of water out of the engine castings. It also helps, I am told, to stop thermostats jamming up because they are dry. This is a moot point, though, and I prefer to drain the cooling system completely. Anti-freeze is a wonderful chemical when mixed with water for finding the tiniest hole in water pipes etc, so do have a minute inspection when this has been added to the cooling system.

It is often necessary to treat larger auxiliary generating engines in the same way as the main engines - lay them up whilst afloat.

3. Loose items such as tools, anchors, outboard motors, etc. may get damaged when craning-out or hauling up a steep slipway: so might mast, standing rigging, stanchions and lifelines. Underwater items such as depth transducers and logs can be knocked off as a yacht swings onto a cradle. Think about the method of hauling out to be used and take action to reduce the possibilities of damage by securing or removal.

4. Deal with the cleansing of the WC holding tank or sanitation tank while facilities at the dockside are there. Some yards have mobile sanitation systems that can come alongside a laid-up boat as well ashore as afloat, but I find the job is usually most easily done while alongside the dock. If you are allowed to discharge the effluent into the sea, make sure this is

done on your last 'engine warming' trip. Several flushes with clean sea-water will really do a power of good to cleanse a holding tank. I then like to fill the tank almost full and put in sufficient formaldehyde solution such as 'Racasan' to purify for a day or two. By then the yacht is ashore, and I take a tank to pump out the solution and leave the system empty and thus free from frost damage. If self-contained heads are to be used in the winter, they can be protected from frost damage by using a suitable anti-freeze in the flushing water tank.

Ashore

1. As the yacht comes out of the water, try to identify the types of marine growth that have fouled her. It will not be the same each season, but over a period of years you can get to know a lot about the degree of fouling to be expected around your mooring or marina and then know what types of anti-fouling are likely to prove most effective. Unless you are having a yard to clean the bottom for you, it is highly advisable to do the scrubbing and cleaning while the fouling is still wet. It will be ten times harder, to say nothing of the smell, if it is left to dry and harden on. Then a tour of inspection is called for. Look at:

a) The state of material the hull is made of. In wood, look for worm attack or the start of softening of the timber, denoting rot. Look particularly along the garboard strake next to the keel. Pay very close attention where paint is showing signs of damage. This may simply be mechanical damage but often failure denotes that something is wrong underneath. In GRP hulls look for blistering below the waterline. This fault has been discussed already (see Chapter 2), but by looking for hull faults now you have plenty of time to rectify them or get the yard onto jobs that call for professional skills. Faults found early will cost money to put to rights, but they will cost less than if they are neglected.

b) Inspect all metal fittings below the waterline for corrosion damage. Look at the split pins on the propeller retaining nuts. It is quite common to find that although these were fitted at the beginning of the season, they are no longer there because they were made of the wrong kind of metal which has now completely corroded away; many propellers are lost because of this. Look at the state of outboard propeller glands in conventional propeller shaft installations, checking corrosion attack and wear. Rubber bearings that are water-lubricated may be allowing the shaft to vibrate; this will accelerate wear and must be seen to. Look to see that inboard bearings that are water-lubricated have been getting a free passage of water down them and that they are thoroughly clear of dried fouling. Look, too, at all the water intakes and outlets on the hull. Clean raw water inlets to the engine cooling system, preferably flushing them with fresh water in the opposite direction from their normal flow. Finally, when everything has dried out a little, do any paint retouching necessary to prevent damage during the winter. Frost and rain getting into a small area that is showing mechanical damage lead to a more serious situation if it is neglected.

2. *Mast, rigging and sails*

Chapter 5 deals in depth with these items but, before de-rigging a yacht, make notes of any repairs and renewal that will need carrying out while the rigging is still *in situ*. Next, make labels and attach them to each piece of rigging as it is removed. It is surprising how much time this will save in identification of parts that need attention and when it comes round to fitting-out time again. The sail-maker has a fairly slack season after lay-up so get the sail directly to him. He will be grateful and will no doubt be able to do a better job, as he will not be rushed off his feet as he is in the spring when everybody wants him to get their sails ready instantly for launching day.

3. *Outboards and outdrives*

Both types of unit will usually have some form of cathodic protection below the waterline. Find them and get replacements if they are needed. Both types of unit should be cleaned with fresh water on the outside. The outboard can be run in a fresh water tank, then both should be dried off. Before cleaning, however, units should be examined for leaking oil seals and damaged glands. The outdrive can give long service, but if water gets into the wrong parts through a rubber gland leaking, expensive damage will result. After inspection, washing and flushing out, the normal winterising procedures referred to in Chapter 6 can proceed.

4. *Batteries and electrical system*

Care of the batteries is referred to in Chapter 7, but the last warming run before laying-up the engine should have ensured that they were in a full state of charge. They should have been topped up to correct electrolyte level before this final charging but, if the level goes down, do ensure there is provision for another charge. Remove batteries to winter storage where charging can take place, as advised. Do not put them in damp, dank places, especially directly onto concrete floors, as in these conditions a leakage of current can occur which will allow sulphating of the plates as the charge goes down. Blocks of wood under the battery will isolate them from a damp floor.

The yacht's electrical wiring needs inspection to see that terminals have not come loose or bared ends broken through embrittlement. Plenty of ventilation will help keep things dry, so open panels containing wiring so that air can circulate. Treat electronic gear as directed in Chapter 7.

5. *Toilet compartment*

This must be left in immaculate condition. Special reference to servicing requirements is referred to in Chapter 8, but your immediate job is to clean the unit and winterise it. If there has been the slightest fault in it during the season or you suspect that anything might be going wrong, now is the time to remove it from the boat and take it home for proper attention. Check skin fitting valves as in Chapter 8. If, like me, you have a dread of launching with the valves still out of place make a large printed 'Launching Safety Check List' and hang it in the cabin to be ticked off in the spring.

6. *Fresh water system*

Freezing water is the chief enemy, for as it expands it will split piping, damage foot valves and ruin a water pump. Two main jobs to be done are thorough cleansing of the system followed by a complete drain down.

7. *Galley*

Again, the galley should be left really clean. It's amazing what a nauseating sight a few crumbs of festering food can present when it has laid in a cupboard all winter! The stove and all around and under it need attention. A paste made up of bicarbonate of soda is great for cleaning stubborn dirt off the inside of the oven and where it has spilled on the top. Next season you can make the job easier by cleaning the oven with a solution of one teaspoonful bicarb, to a pint of water and leaving this to dry on; dirt will then come off much easier next time a major clean is necessary. Fridges go smelly if they are left unventilated. The same weak solution of bicarb. will cleanse them after defrosting. This time, though, dry the clean surface. I have made a shock cord fastening for my fridge door so that it is held open to allow ventilation but will not swing about and do itself and surrounding furniture a mischief.

8. *Safety Equipment*

All equipment should be removed to dry storage, inspected and serviced. The last two are jobs for the quiet winter months. Some equipment, such as life-rafts and life-jackets, will require professional attention and the sooner this can be handed over the better will the servicing firm be pleased, as business is usually slack at this time of the year. The most horrific things can and do happen to life-rafts that are not properly looked after and which do not receive their annual servicing.

Flares become outdated and need to be disposed of. The coastguard will usually arrange disposal, but I must admit I find one of the national celebrations where fireworks are used an ideal time to familiarise myself and crew with the working of pyrotechnics. You need this confidence in an emergency and provided they are not seriously outdated the operation will be safe. These are not - repeat NOT - for the children to play with.

Any safety equipment using batteries - emergency radio beacon, life-jacket lights and dan pole lights - should have the batteries removed. The old batteries can be used for household purposes and new ones bought for the emergency appliances next season. While work goes on aboard, fire extinguishers should always be in place. When the covers go on is the time to have them serviced.

9. *Hull, topsides and deck equipment*

Whatever material your yacht is built from a thorough wash down with clean water will remove dirt and, in the case of sea-going craft, salt. When all is dry, touching up damaged surfaces will protect them from water and frost damage. If you are lucky to get a really warm autumn day, this is ideal for the job, but don't worry if things are less than ideal so long as the substrata is day and the paint goes onto this. GRP can have temporary touching-up done above the waterline but below, the material needs some time to dry out thoroughly before repairs can be attempted. Varnish work must be rubbed down in damaged areas and a couple of coats given for protection. It doesn't matter how rough it is, as you will be rubbing down again in the spring, so if damp makes it go dull don't worry.

Check all deck fittings to see that they are not coming adrift and that they will not allow any water into the hull via their fastenings. It is vital to see that the boat is plumb in her normal attitude or that she will allow any rain water lodging on her to drain off every part. I have seen fuel tanks flooded with rain water simply because it seeped into them as a pool covered the deck fitting cap. See that the tank top gasket is sound and renew if necessary. Do the same for the fresh water tank filler cap.

Deck machinery, anchor windlass and sailboat sheet winches only need cleaning and given the maker's recommended winterisation treatment. Each maker will have specific recommendations, especially for oils and greases to be used. If he names a specific oil or grease, he does so for very good reasons. If any mechancial faults are present, this equipment should be removed from the deck and taken home to a workshop.

10. *Winter covers*

With all loose equipment removed, every part of the yacht's mechanical system winterised and every part of the yacht cleaned and polished, the last operation is to put on the winter covers. The following points must receive consideration.

Covers will chafe deck structures if they are not properly protected. Rope chafe from a gale will seriously damage both wood and GRP, so meticulous attention needs to be given to this problem. Scrap materials found round the home can help. Old tights and stockings tied round rope where it will chafe, rubber carpet backing wound round stanchions, pulpit and pushpits will stop chafe to the cover. Off-cuts of cushion foam or even old cushions in polythene bags to prevent them absorbing water, will raise the winter cover off the pressure points on cabin and wheelhouse tops and, incidentally, allow passage of ventilating air under the cover.

The mast is often used as a ridge pole for the winter cover. This is ideal provided it is properly supported and the mast fittings covered to prevent chafe. Trestles are easily made with crossed battens either lashed or bolted together just below where the ridge pole will rest. Deck cleats can be used for the ropes that will act as guys to the trestles (Fig. 19).

A Norwegian acquaintance of mine is fortunate to have several million larch trees growing at the bottom of his garden, and he simply lops enough to make a perfect ridge tent, covers it with thick polythene and drapes a net over the lot to hold it in place. Winter covering for most of us, however, will be more expensive though well worth-while. Covers may be made out of the following materials.

a) **Cotton ducks**, 12oz weight for small craft, 15 or 18 oz for larger covers. Its advantage as a cover is that while remaining waterproof it does 'breathe', allowing condensation to escape. It will rip right across if a gale gets under it and it must be waterproofed with a wax emulsion brushed hard into it every season if it is not to have a very limited life.

b) **Flax** makes a strong cover but is not as long-lasting as cotton duck as it is more vulnerable to chafe. It is very flexible and will not rip right across if a tear develops. Again, waterproofing solutions should be used. The firms that make up covers will usually advise on the treatments they have found successful.

c) **PVC impregnated fabrics.** These are often plasticised jute and are very strong but prone to delamination and cracking on chafe lines. They do not need proofing so long as damage can be avoided, but patching needs to be kept up where damage occurs. Like all plastics, they do not 'breathe' so special care is required to see that ventilating spaces are adequate beneath them.

d) **Polythene and polythene impregnated nettings.** Polythene itself is very inexpensive but will be blown to tatters in no time if there is any flapping or chafe. It is a complete waste of time unless a net is used to cover it: then only heavy duty 'building' grades should be chosen. It is the very devil to

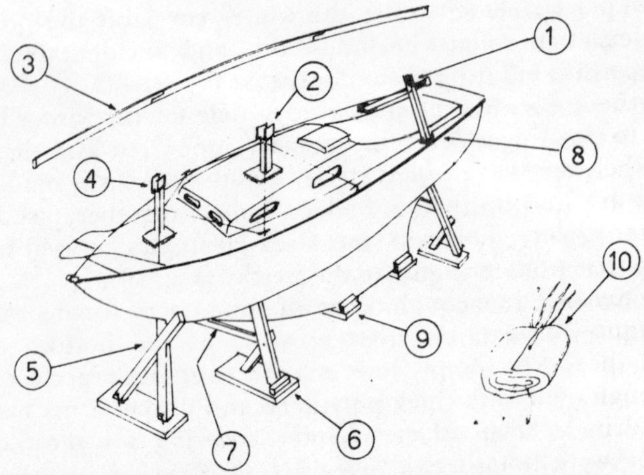

1. Leather crutch mast supports.
2. Single guyed support on foam.
3. Wood ridge pole in sections.
4. Mast supports must be level
5. All overhangs supported.
6. Legs must be dogged.
7. Legs tied.
8. Plastic foam padding under.
9. Blocks, dogged, to level hull.
10. Re-Proofed cover, check ropes.
11. Steel cradle for max. safety.
12. Remove propellers - security.
13. Seal off all deck fittings.
14. Check all skin fittings.
15. Check cathodic protection.
16. Make good damage.
17. Check steering & rudders.
18. Foam pad all hard spots.

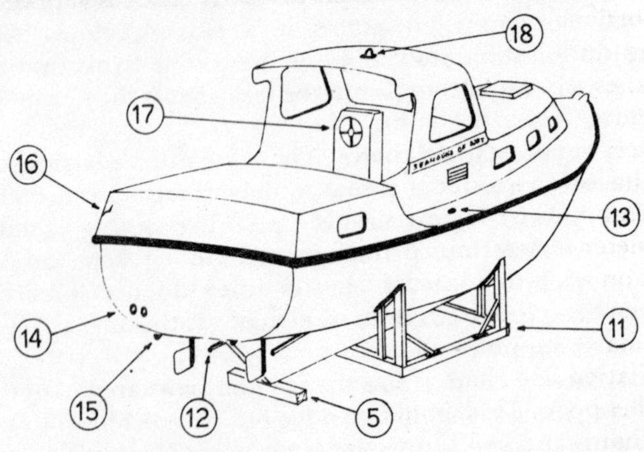

Fig.19. Winter Lay-up

get in place if there is a breath of wind and I don't like the way condensation collects under it. Nettings are stronger, quite inexpensive but otherwise suffer from the same disadvantages. Polythene does not rot but is sometimes vulnerable to UV light and to cracking in low temperatures.

It helps preserve winter covers of any kind if the bows of the boat are laid up in the direction of the strongest prevailing winter gales. There is something wrong with the cover supporting system if pools form! Get this seen to as the weight of water will damage or even rip the cover. If it freezes it may do equal damage. It is often advocated in maintenance books that the cover should have openings at bow and stern for through ventilation purposes. The problem here is that rain can drive in from either end and snow will get in as though the cover were not there at all. A solution is to get some 6in (15.5cm) diameter soft plastic pipe, such as that used to conduct air round an air-blown domestic central heating system, and rig it with lines over the gunwale. The winter cover drawn down over these will allow air to blow up the hull sides and through them.

11. *Security and insurance*

It is a sad reflection of the times we live in that yachts are increasingly becoming the targets for vandals and thieves. Losses and vandalism on craft afloat is reaching unwelcome proportions but once ashore your pride and joy becomes a sitting duck rather than a boat. That is why all removable items, especially outboard motors and electronic gear, should be removed before coming ashore, or, if more convenient, on the very same day she comes onto dry land. Any stepladders you have for climbing aboard must always be locked up, preferably away from the boat itself. It is true that nothing will deter a determined thief, but at least we can make him work on a job that much longer and this time spells security as he then has a greater chance of being caught.

I have emphasised the need to provide really good ventilation and there is a temptation to leave ports, doors and hatches open. This should be done only if you can also arrange for chains and locks to secure them in such a way that a thief or vandal cannot enter. Eye-bolts with short lengths of chain and padlocks are a simple and effective remedy. There are self-powered burglar alarm systems available which sound an alarm when a pressure pad or switch is involuntarily operated. These are all well and good in populated areas but so often craft are laid up in isolated places - still, they will give the would-be thief something to think about. Propellers are expensive items and fetch good value as scrap. Their removal for safe storage is therefore advocated. Thieves have been known to saw through shafts to get them off.

Contact your insurance company so that an understanding is reached regarding items stored at home or away from the yacht.

12. *Miscellaneous items*

I list the yacht tender for priority attention. If it can be taken home all the better, for it can be dried out and on one of those shocking wet weekends in the dead of winter it can provide you with just sufficient work to whet the appetite for spring and the joys of a season ahead.

Inflatables should be laid up by washing thoroughly and checking that small grit and sand is cleared from the join at the floor and side tubes.

The transom of wood should be rubbed down and painted or varnished. Clean the valves and do any patching that is necessary.

Wooden tenders need the same care as wooden boats so check for rot, repair and then paint. Pay real attention to areas round rowlocks where the most stress and wear takes place.

Repair that rubber rubbing strake so that the yacht topsides will not be damaged by projecting screws! Look under the tender to see if worn rubbing strakes need renewing. As the tender grates onto the concrete hard on coming ashore, it's hardly a wonder that the strakes need frequent renewal. This kind of treatment is death to a GRP tender unless really first-class rubbing strakes are designed so that the GRP is not abraded. I had my own plywood tender 'Cascover' sheathed underneath and, although it added weight, it is in perfect condition after twelve years' service and has been painted only once over the sheathing in that time. If the tender rides on davits, check that these are laid up properly by cleaning with water, touching up damaged paint where applicable and oiling or greasing mechanical parts.

Upholstery and curtains should be removed from the damp and washed or dry-cleaned. Large polythene storage bags are often available from the cleaners and they can have a moth repellent added before they are sealed up for the winter and stored in a dry place.

Chapter 10
FITTING-OUT PROCEDURES

Ashore

1. Winter covers.
2. Cleaning down.
3. Painting.
4. Preparing engines for use.
5. Preparing domestic systems for use – water, toilet and cooking stoves.
6. Trailers.
7. Rigging.
8. Cradles.

Afloat

1. Checking moorings and insurance.
2. Starting and checking engines.
3. Running and sailing trials.
4. Instrument calibration.

If you really went to town on the winterisation programme and have got all the repairs done that were on your lay-up list, you should now have a flying start to the exciting business of fitting-out for the new season. To be honest, I like to have all the repairs done before the spring and I am fortunate to have an understanding yard where I can have a power supply ashore right through the winter so that heat and power for electric tools is always to hand. The dry heat from a fan heater does a power of good for the interior and keeps me comfortable while small refurbishing jobs go on. But I still look forward to the stirring of the blood when the winter covers come off and the season's fitting-out begins.

Ashore

1. *The winter cover*
Before you get carried away, chalk-mark all the holes that have been leaking or where patches will have to be put over chafed areas and get it round immediately to the sailmaker for repairs. Duck covers can be reproofed in the early spring when it may be too blustery for painting but fine enough for drying a wax emulsion such as 'Mesowax', made by Grangersol. Light canvas awnings, dodgers and sail covers can be treated with 'Fabsil', made by the same company, which will make them mildew-resistant as well as waterproofing them. Fabsil is a colourless silicone solution and can be used on interior upholstery quite safely.
2. *Cleaning down*
You will be surprised at the amount of dirt blown aboard by the winter gales and carried aboard by muddy boots. If there is a hosepipe and plentiful water supply all the better, as dirt is better soaked before the scrubbing brush is produced. This washing down applies to all types of boats. My own boat always seems to be near oily soot-polluted air from various sources these days. The cleaning down is important as it will allow the glasspaper to bite in better when you are rubbing down a wooden boat, and it will allow you to see the real condition of things as you slowly scrub away.
3. *Painting*
This is so important that I gave it a chapter early on all to itself. The loving care that is put in is always repaid when you realise how good yachts maintain their value.
4. *Preparing engines*
This is again a matter of visual inspection and cleaning off. Preservatives that have been brushed onto the engine can be cleaned down with white spirit. Engines and drives are going to be the biggest job after painting, so here goes.
a) **Lubrication system.** Pump out preservative oils if used and replenish with the correct grade recommended oil. Check

levels in every part of the unit, not forgetting out-drive gears, gearboxes, reduction gears, and those required by the outboard motor. In any engine where oil has been put into the cylinder you must be quite certain it is blown out or a hydraulic lock could bend a connecting rod and even push it through the side of the crankcase. Wait for this until you have the cooling system full on on inboard engines and then, as with other types, place a cloth over the plug or injector holes and use the starter or a smart hand turn to blow out excess oil. See that seatings for plugs or injectors are clean and then replace with the correctly serviced units.

b) **Cooling systems.** If laid up 'dry', check that all valves and drain taps or plugs are closed or replaced. Plugs should be greased so that they will come out next time and taps should be oiled. If 'wet' winterisation was used on an indirect system, check minutely for any leaks that might have developed. Anti-freeze solutions are the very devil for finding the smallest gap in a system, but this is not a bad thing for safety as it is then easily remedied. Both oil and cooling system levels are only roughly checked at this stage as the craft may well be out of level compared to her floating level. Final checks must be done when afloat.

Replace the Jabsco type impeller and put a new gasket on before screwing the end plate in place.

c) Take all sealing tape off carburettors, air intakes or breather pipes that you might have sealed up.

d) The electrical system needs the batteries replacing if they have been removed. Connect the battery leads with the correct polarity and smear them with petroleum jelly. Check that they have already been topped up and fully charged. Turn on the battery master switch and observe voltmeters if you have them.

e) Make sure you have enough fuel aboard to get you to the fuelling berth. Check over all fuel lines and filters to ensure there are still no leaks.

f) Check that the propeller is properly secured. Check that drive shafts are free by turning them by hand.

g) Touch up any paint on the engine after you have gone over all nuts to see they are secure. Check every hose clip.

h) Outboard portable fuel tanks must have their fuel line connectors checked and the proper grade petrol/oil mixture added. Check that tank holding straps, if fitted, are in good condition.

The aim for any type of engine installation is to have it ready to start almost the moment the boat hits the water.

5. *Preparing domestic systems*

The first job always is to install the yacht's fire fighting equipment, serviced during the winter. You are going to check galley stove, electrical systems and engines so this is sensible, just in case there is trouble.

Check out the gas system by means of a washing-up liquid applied at every single joint. Make sure the gas bottle is turned on and look for bubbles. Joints must always be made with new olives and 'Calortite' jointing compound if a leak is found. Other stoves should be lighted up and tested as it is much easier to get them off again by car than to have to run them ashore when afloat. Do not test water heating systems without the tanks and pipes being full! Bleed off the air in pipes before lighting up.

Water tanks, cleaned out earlier, can now be filled. If you are not near a tap, just enough water is needed to enable you to test the water system - pumps, foot-valves, heaters, taps, etc. Check that all taps are off, the system is, if needed, primed and that the electric supply is on. With pressurised systems, the pump will soon get the head of water it operates on and then shut off. Opening the tap will allow pressure to drop and the pressure switch will start the pump again. When pressurised, see that any system has not been damaged by frost, that no pipes are leaking and no taps dripping. On simple galley water supplies, using a hand pump soon tests the system and gets it working.

Many yachts now have a fresh water filtration system and, before filling, filter elements may need to be replaced. I have 'hot', 'cold' and 'for whisky' taps, the latter supply being fed through an Ogden Aquaflow purifying filter; this unit ceases to flow when it needs replacing.

6. *Trailer care*

Fig. 20 indicates the main points that need attention. If the boat has lain on a jacked-up trailer all winter, now is the time to check out wheel bearing and braking systems. The wheel should have been removed for the winter and you should now

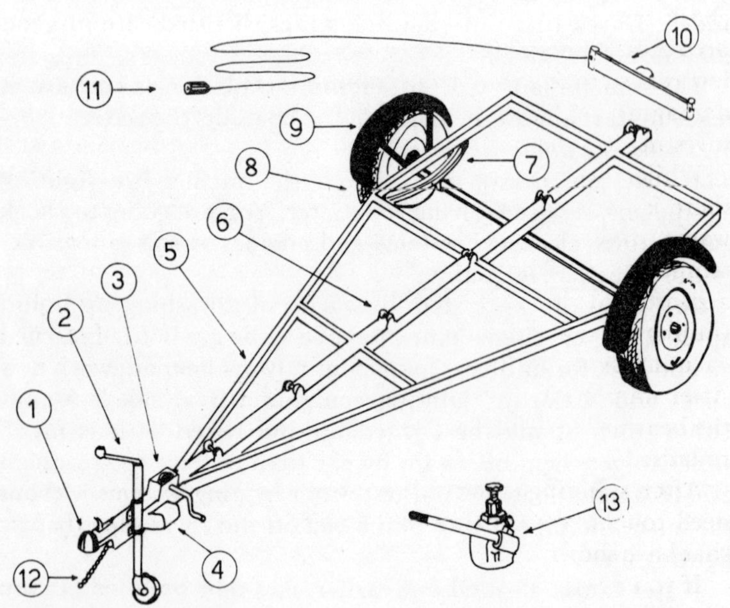

1. Ball hitch – grease – lock.
2. Jocky wheel
3. Winch – check pawls, wire rope.
4. Braking system.
5. Paint chassis.
6. Rollers – see they do.
7. Suspension – treat correctly.
8. Tyres – tread, pressure, loading.
9. Mudguards.
10. Number & brake light bulbs.
11. Electrical connectors.
12. Safety chain & fixing points.
13. Jack – service – do not overload.
14. Brake linings & mechanism
15. Oil seals.
16. Inner bearing.
17. Outer bearing.
18. 'D' Washer.
19. Stub end nut & split pin.
20. Hub cap

BE AWARE OF LAW RELATING TO BOAT TRAILERS

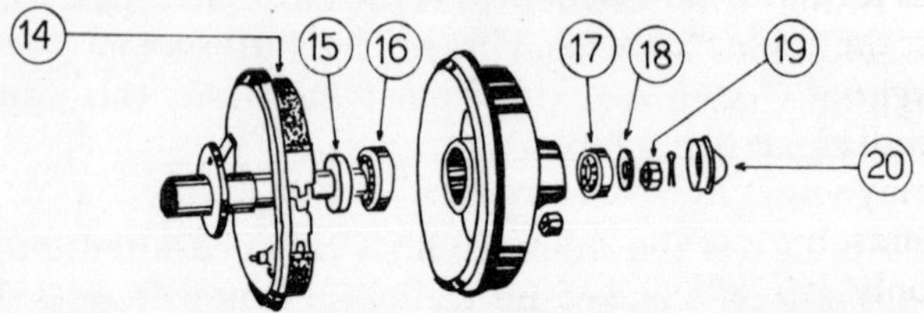

Fig.20. Trailer Servicing Points

check tyre tread (which must comply with the law) and tyre pressures. Most people know that oil will damage tyres, but few realise that strong sunlight and seaside ozone are equally damaging. A canvas cover for trailer wheels is a good investment if the trailer is to stand on a hard for the summer.

While the tyres are off, look over the wheel bearings. If there is the slightest doubt that they have been damaged by water, replace and thoroughly grease them with a high temperature wheel bearing grease. The problem is accentuated because wheel bearings run hot even when trailing a short distance, and when they are immersed a vacuum is created as they cool and water is sucked into them. After immersion, fresh grease should always be pumped into the bearings to drive out the water – something seldom actually practised.

After standing about all winter, the trailer chassis might need touching up with a metal primer over any rust patches that have shown up.

If you do use a trailer for your boat, make yourself familiar with all the legal requirements necessary. Check the lighting. Connect cables and with the aid of a friend see that braking lights, number plate illuminators and direction indicators are in working order. Check cables for chafe.

Hydraulic servo assist braking systems should be serviced by a professional, but you can inspect the mechanism for any signs of oil leakage. Flexible hoses used in some systems should be replaced immediately any signs of deterioration, such as swell or chafe, show. Have the air bled from these brakes after repairs or servicing. See that the ball hitch is well greased and that the hitch assembly on the trailer is working smoothly.

Desmo Ltd. have recently brought out a balance which makes it easy to measure the weight on the ball hitch and then adjust the trailer loading. This will help prevent snaking.

7. *Rigging*

Depending on the type of boat and the launching facilities, this may sometimes be completed before launching. Assuming that mast maintenance has been completed during the winter, the only job left is to step it and make fast the standing rigging. The stepping will be an exact opposite of the procedures you went through for taking down the mast

(Chapter 5). Rigging screws must be carefully adjusted to the same 'tune' as the previous season. The really keen sailing man will of course fine tune the mast when on sailing trials, but getting it near the mark will help. If you take dimensions by measuring the angle made between boom and mast, then distance from boom end to some fixed point under it in the cockpit, provided you note them down, say in the log book, you have a good start when re-rigging. Make sure every split pin is inserted in rigging screws so that it cannot tear an unsuspecting finger! Stainless steel safety rings are better for small clevis fastenings and shackles can be moused with monel seizing wire. If the mast is ever to go over the side, it will usually be because one of the end fittings has failed. Have another visual check to see that none of them are below par before parcelling them up in either a canvas bag or one of these new-fangled plastic slip-on fittings that will keep out the weather and stop chafe.

Stanchions may have been removed from their bases for the winter. You will already have seen that bases are safe at the painting stage, but now see that the split pins are inserted in every base to secure the stanchion. Badly distorted pins may be driven in, to be regretted later in the year when they will be the very devil to remove. They don't cost much, so when they are getting badly bent renew them.

Lifelines are rigged next, and remember they mean what they say. Inspect every inch of them again and look especially at end fittings. See that they are 'safety rigged' by putting in new split pins when the rigging screws have been properly tensioned.

8. *Cradles*

Assuming the boat has been taken to the water and is now safely afloat, do spare a moment for the cradle she might have been resting on during the winter. I find a cradle much more convenient and safer than using legs and shores. It should be treated to an epoxy painting every other year. The rubber coverings at the four main resting points should be renewed as necessary and then it can be put away for the summer at the yard.

Afloat

1. Afloat again, you'll be glad you asked the boatman to check the mooring! Pulling up a laden buoy and rusty chain onto your pristine decks is not the way to start the season. Your insurance company would not appreciate this lackadaisical attitude at all and, in fact, they will hold you responsible for the safety of your mooring. It is well worth looking at your mooring contracts to see just who is responsible if a summer gale carries your boat away. Again, it is a simple courtesy to drop your insurance company a line to tell them your craft is afloat, for although it is generally accepted that a season starts around a certain date, you may have launched earlier and have no cover in law. I have never known an insurance company dispute this point, but the risk of testing its legality is really not to be recommended.

2. *Starting and checking engines*

a) Do the final check on oil and coolant levels.

b) See that dipsticks and coolant caps have been replaced and no drain cocks are leaking.

c) Turn on raw water supply at the skin-fitting sea-cock and check there is no ingress of water. I dread to mention some old craft I have seen which take water through the planking till they swell up and the seams become tight again. Check all sea-cocks through the boat to see that they were indeed closed at the last land-check and that no water is entering anywhere.

d) Turn on the battery master switch or switches and, if you have them, the circuit-breakers.

e) Run up any ventilation fans for five minutes, especially if they are in the engine compartment.

f) Check that engine controls are free and gearbox is in neutral.

g) On diesel engines, use the cold start and *press* the button to breath new life into those treasured units once again.

h) If nothing happens, don't go on torturing the starter motor. Check out basic functions like the fuel system being primed, chokes open on petrol motors, and after a rest try again. The odds are, if you are keen enough to have done all the suggested homework, the engine will soon start.

j) When it has started inspect for oil and water leaks. It could be a gasket has gone askew when reassembling a filter, so a thorough inspection is again carried out while the engines are run up to temperature. When all is well, stop the engine and check out the sails if you have a sail boat.

3. *Running trials*

For the first few hours of every season the yachtsman will check out that equipment is functioning perfectly and spend some time checking each mechanical part of the yacht. Cruising is spoiled later in the season if the skipper has to be doing one repair and maintenance job after another. Listen that while under way the shafting is running sweetly, that sails hoist easily and sail slides run true and easily in their tracks. There really is a sense of joy and achievement if everything is near as dammit perfect.

4. *Instrument calibration*

Before accurate dead reckoning navigation can be achieved, it is necessary to know the error of the instruments being used, and at the beginning of each season one would be well advised to check and recalibrate instruments as accurately as possible.

Depth sounders may or may not have facilities for instrument calibration, but it is an easy matter to have an accurately marked lead over the side in 5 metres or so. Check the sounder against the true depth and adjust the instrument or note its true error in the log book.

Log and speedometer. You must have a stretch of water where the distance between two points is known and transit marks are available. Measured miles are sometimes marked but not always conveniently close. Choose a time when there's only a light wind and use the motor at its standard cruising rpm. Calibrate at a time when the stream is at a settled rate, neither near slack nor high water. The speed of the current should be known so that if needed a correction factor can be applied to calculations. If the ship speed is greater than ten, no correction is necessary; if it is less than ten, the correction factors shown opposite will be needed.

These errors can sometimes be reduced by calibration screws as provided on Brooks & Gatehouse 'Harrier', otherwise the errors are noted in the navigation log book.

Calibration of speedometer. Do runs between transits at the yacht's usual cruising speed. Use a stop-watch to time the runs

Ship Speed—Speed of Current	10	7	6	5	4.5	4
Correction Factor	1.01	1.02	1.03	1.04	1.05	1.07

Example 1 Listed distance between two transits = 6,080 ft (one nautical mile)

Run down stream indicated by log = 0.95 n.m.
Run up stream indicated by log = 1.01 n.m.

Total = 1.96 n.m.

2 nautical miles—1.96 n.m. = 0.04 n.m. error or 2 per cent under reading

$$\frac{\text{Ship Speed}}{\text{Speed of Current}} = \frac{1.01 + 0.95}{1.01 - 0.95} = \frac{1.96}{0.06} = 32 \text{ approx.}$$ No correction

Example 2 Listed distance between transits = 6,080 ft (one nautical mile)

Run down stream indicated by log = 1.19 n.m.
Run up stream indicated by log = 0.92 n.m.

2.11 n.m.

$$\frac{\text{Ship Speed}}{\text{Speed of Current}} = \frac{1.19 + 0.92}{1.19 - 0.92} = \frac{2.11}{0.27} = 7.8 \text{ approx.}$$ Correction on table needed:

Correction Factor to Distance Sailed = 2 n.m. x 1.015 (Interpolate from table)
= 2.03 n.m.

Error = 2.11 - 2.03 = 0.08 n.m. or 4 per cent over reading

and then calibrate the speedometer. It is essential to maintain a given speed in each direction, so either choose a day with calm or increase engine rpm to hold speed into wind.

Time Upstream = 11 minutes for 1 n.m. = 5.5 knots
Time Downstream = 9 minutes for 1 n.m. = 6.5 knots

$$\text{Speed through water} = \frac{5.5 + 6.5}{2} = \frac{12}{2} = 6 \text{ knots}$$

The instrument read-out should be calibrated to read this value or discrepancy noted in the navigation log book; Reed's 'Speed Tables' are useful.

Finally, swing that compass. If you have established your own reliable transits in the harbour, 'swinging ship' is a straightforward procedure. However, alterations made during the winter might just have created greater deviation than previously; if this is so, the services of a qualified compass adjuster are recommended. With faith in the compass, a seaworthy craft you can equally trust in, you are all set for another happy boating season.

INDEX